Making Love Stay

❦

Also by James and Peggy Vaughan:
Beyond Affairs
Also by James Vaughan:
Please Trust Me
Also by Peggy Vaughan:
The Monogamy Myth

❦

Making ❦ *Love*

❦ *Stay* ❦

Insights and Affirmations
for Romance and Relationships

Peggy Vaughan
and
James Vaughan, Ph.D.

HarperSanFrancisco
A Division of HarperCollins*Publishers*

MAKING LOVE STAY: *Insights and Affirmations for Romance and Relationships.* Coyright © 1993 by Peggy Vaughan and James Vaughan, Ph.D. All rights reserved. Printed in the United States of America. No part of this book may be used or reproduced in any manner whatsoever without written permission except in the case of brief quotations embodied in critical articles and reviews. For information address HarperCollins Publishers, 10 East 53rd Street, New York, NY 10022.

Reprinted by arrangement with Lowell House, a division of RGA Publishing Group, Inc.

FIRST HARPERCOLLINS PAPERBACK EDITION PUBLISHED IN 1994

Library of Congress Cataloging-in-Publication Data
Vaughan, Peggy.
    Making love stay : insights and affirmations for romance and relationships /Peggy Vaughan and James Vaughan. — 1st HarperCollins pbk. ed.
        p. cm.
    Originally published: Making love stay: everything you ever knew about love but forgot. Los Angeles: Lowell House:
Chicago: Contemporary Books, © 1992.
        ISBN 0-06-250919-5 (pb : acid-free paper)
        1. Man-woman relationships. 2. Love. 3. Interpersonal communication. I. Vaughan, James A. II. Title.
HQ801.V34   1994
306.7-dc20   92-56120
                                                            CIP

94 95 96 97 98 ❖ BANTA 10 9 8 7 6 5 4 3 2 1

This edition is printed on acid-free paper that meets the American National Standards Institute Z39.48 Standard.

Contents

Making Love Stay

The Challenge of Making Love Stay

*A*re you frustrated by the endless stream of suggestions for magically improving your love life—like having sex in strange places or going to motels with no luggage? Are you tired of trying all the gimmicks and tricks that make you feel foolish or embarrassed—like Saran Wrap surprises, wearing no underwear, or talking dirty on the phone? Are you discouraged by seeing that these tricks don't seem to work the way you hope they will—or that they only work temporarily and then you're right back where you started?

If you're feeling desperate and doomed to a life of struggling to find and keep a good relationship, don't give up hope. You can have a lasting love. And it doesn't require any miracles. Deep down you know everything you need to know about making love last;

you just forgot. What you need to do is calmly reflect on what you already know—and then act on it. That's what this book will help you do.

We have been continually frustrated by the simplistic techniques offered in many books and the superficial views about love propagated by the media. Love is far too serious and significant in our lives to be given such short shrift. So we're offering a guide with substance (the meat-and-potatoes approach) as opposed to the superficial approach that deals only with the image of a good marriage and only with the surface issues.

This is a guidebook, an instruction manual, and a source of inspiration whenever you get discouraged. You can't pick up this book and not find something you can use. And while it may not seem sexy, if you consistently follow its suggestions, it will do more for your sex life than any sex manual you can buy.

The ideas in this book come straight from our own experience—both personally and professionally. We've been married for 37 years and have spent the past 20 years working with hundreds of other couples on their relationship issues. These experiences have brought us a new clarity about what's important in making love last. But you don't have to take our word for it; you can verify the ideas in this book from your own experience.

You'll see that this stuff is not pie in the sky. It's very basic and solid. And since it grew directly out of our own struggles to make love stay, it's based on reality. We faced most of the problems that any couple faces. We didn't have insight into how to avoid them (or how to deal with them if we couldn't avoid them), but we survived—and we learned from our experiences.

Looking back, we can see how desperately we needed a book like this when we were starting out. So we've written the book we should have had but didn't. We know a lot of you are bogged down in the same kinds of thinking we were and facing some of the same issues we faced. But you don't have to stay frustrated and disappointed about the course of your love. You do have this book, and you can use it to make your love stay.

Inspiring You to Take Charge of Your Life

Falling in love is easy, but staying in love is quite another matter. Apparently it's one of the most difficult things any of us ever attempts. Because of the high divorce rate and the large percentage of remaining marriages in which couples don't have a vital love relationship, you may have come to believe it's inevitable that love will fade with time. Or perhaps you've already experienced the discouragement of seeing the love you once shared somehow slip away.

Don't settle for thinking that you really can't expect more. You can and you should—regardless of your current situation. While no long-term love relationship is without difficulties, it *is* possible for love to survive and to be renewed and transformed over time. That's what this book is about—showing you how you can realistically aspire to something better.

Relationships can be the source of great joy or great pain. They seldom stand still; they're either getting better or getting worse. You deserve more out of love than just a few brief romantic interludes or an ongoing struggle simply to get along. You don't want life to pass you by while you're waiting (and hoping) for a good relationship. You'll feel better if you're actively doing something toward that end. By paying attention to what's happening—and taking responsibility for what's happening—you can make a difference.

If you still doubt whether you can direct the course of your love, maybe you'll find encouragement by hearing a little bit about our own struggles to change the course of our love. Even where the specifics of our experiences are unlike yours, the similarity of the struggle is a connection we all share.

When we married at age 19, we had no real concept of what was involved in making love stay. We believed our love was so special that it could withstand anything. Like most couples, we tended to take our relationship for granted and to forget everything we knew was necessary to keep our love strong. Through the years we confronted many of the standard problems that can drive a wedge between partners if they aren't paying attention.

For instance, early in our marriage we found ourselves involved in one of the most common problems of all—losing touch with each other because we focused so much on career and children. We lost touch not because we were focusing on other areas but because we didn't talk straight to each other about how we felt about the situation.

We just went along, thinking this was the way things had to be. We didn't realize that you don't have to change your circumstances; you only have to change how you deal with them. Unfortunately, we simply didn't deal with them. So we became distant from each other—and lost that deep connection that's critical to making love stay.

The weakening of our basic connection made us vulnerable to all kinds of other problems that affect long-term relationships. One of the most common is simply the familiarity that comes from being together over the years. We started taking each other for granted—seeing each other primarily as husband and wife instead of as individuals.

This shift in our thinking was gradual—we didn't even realize it was happening. We fell into sexually stereotyping each other as one of "them." This included a lot of "ain't it awful" thinking, as in, "Men are so distant, so preoccupied with their own interests, so insensitive, so uncommunicative," and on the other side, "Women are so emotional, so smothering, so demanding, so talkative."

Naturally, each of us thought we were right in our assessment of what was wrong with the other. And commiserating with others only reinforced these stereotypical ways of reacting to each other. Slowly but surely, we joined the masses who view the opposite sex not as individuals but as members of a mysterious group that you don't understand and can't change—so you just have to tolerate. This attitude further increased the distance between us and weakened the loving aspect of our relationship.

These standard problems became like a cancer, slowly robbing us of the closeness we had originally felt. Our love wasn't gone, but it was suffocating under the mounting pressure of fulfilling our roles while losing ourselves.

What finally got our attention was a crisis—the issue of extramarital affairs. It shook us to the core and forced us to learn, or *relearn*, many of the basic principles we had forgotten. We had thought we were good communicators because we did talk. We had never fallen into the trap of using the silent treatment to deal with differences, but it was only when we were confronted with a situation that required some really deep talk that we began to learn to communicate effectively.

Understanding how and why we had gotten to that point, working through the hurt, and rebuilding trust gave us a new appreciation of the healing power of honest communication. Since that point—almost 20 years ago—we have consistently tried to implement the ideas and suggestions we're now offering to you. We know these ideas work because our love and trust are now deeper and stronger than ever—solidly based on a shared, ongoing commitment to honesty and fairness.

We're not holding ourselves up as a perfect couple. On the contrary, we fully expect to continue learning and working on our relationship. We still have high expectations of love, but they're based on experience and realistic possibilities rather than magical thinking.

We invite you to use our insights, not as the final answers to your problems but as a means of helping you find your own answers. You have the power to make your love last—and this book can help you do it.

Of course, the title of this book is misleading if you take it literally; you can't arbitrarily and unilaterally make love do anything. On the other hand, love doesn't come and go capriciously. This book is about what you can do that will make all the difference in whether or not your love will stay.

Understanding Love and Its Place in Your Life
Throughout the book we'll be giving you specific actions to help make your love stay—but you really

need a clear understanding of some basic ideas before you start. The thing to understand is what's at stake. We're not talking about some little fringe issue in your life here. When all is said and done, having a long-term, loving relationship ranks near the top of the list of the best of what life has to offer.

This book is different from most others in that it respects love's significance. We are presenting a way of looking at your love relationship in the context of your life as a whole. Our goal is to help you achieve a love that provides a solid place to stand in the world. Your love can be the kind of positive force that lets you go out and face the world on a completely different basis than you could do otherwise.

In focusing on this goal, we are trying to avoid the pitfalls of the romantic approach to making love stay. We're elevating the meaning of a loving relationship beyond just achieving temporary pleasure. Part of our motivation for writing this book came from our growing concern with the popular advice that's based on this shortsighted, superficial approach to sustaining (or reviving) love.

This is a book of substance for people who want the most from what love has to offer. It's simple without being simplistic, and it's serious without being stuffy. We are suggesting a wide range of interconnected actions that are based on a deep understanding of the nature of lasting love.

The Changing Nature of Love

The first step in making love stay is to understand that lasting love is not the same as the exciting, heady feeling of falling in love. Love changes; it never remains the same—and trying to keep it from changing is sure to snuff it out.

Let's follow the course of love as you're likely to experience it. First, you fall in love. What a wonderful feeling! It's intoxicating and all-consuming. You can't think of anything else—and you can't keep your hands off each other. (Personally, we still refer to the beginning of our own relationship at age 17 as our period of "young, hot love"—but, of course, these feelings aren't restricted to young people; they're typical of any new love at any age.)

Falling in love, or "new love," produces some of the most intense feelings you will ever experience. At its best, it seems too good to be real. It is real, but it won't last—at least not in that form. Enjoy new love for the fantastic experience that it is, but recognize that much of the intensity of the feeling is inherent in its newness and novelty. You may wish these feelings would never end, and you may go to any length to sustain them or to rekindle them when you feel them changing. But the popular tricks and gimmicks for maintaining that particular kind of excitement are doomed to fail.

While romantic touches are wonderful for stimulating exciting lovemaking and adding spice to your relationship, they aren't sufficient by themselves to build a lasting love. They may give your relationship a temporary shot in the arm—but it will quickly fade and you'll be right back where you started. This superficial approach just won't work over the long haul.

If the romantic fix doesn't work, you may wonder why there are so many books and so much advice about how to recapture the first flush of love and put the *zing* back in your marriage. Well, it's really not too hard to figure out. In a couple of key ways, that kind of advice about love is a lot like the books and advice about crash diets; it's based on the fantasy that there's a quick and easy way to do it.

Just as you can quickly lose some weight with a crash diet, you can quickly create a spark in your relationship with a sexy gimmick. Just as it's much easier to go on a specified diet for a specified period of time than to change your overall eating habits for life, it's also easier to pursue some specific sexual encounters than to change your overall ways of relating for life. But in both cases, this approach doesn't last. With the diet, you wind up regaining the weight and feeling even worse than before. And with your relationship, the temporary surge of feelings inevitably fades and things settle back to the way they were before (or worse), and you wind up feeling more discouraged than ever.

Every failed attempt at reviving the feelings of new love further diminishes the hope that anything will work. At some point, you need to say no to these yo-yo tactics and get serious about making real change. If you feel like saying, "I'm mad as hell and I'm not going to take it anymore," then you're ready for this book and its solid, long-term approach to making love stay.

Letting Go of Myths

One of the biggest myths about love is the idea that love never changes. Unfortunately, you sabotage your chances for lasting love if you think that the feelings associated with falling in love are the ultimate in loving. Romantic love is just the first stage of love, and it either evolves into a deeper, richer love or it withers. Rejecting this myth is the only way to move beyond the initial stage of love to achieve the richness that's possible in a loving relationship. To make love stay, you must face your fear of losing it and consciously support the transition from new to lasting love.

Lasting love is not a less desirable state; it's just different. It has its own unique form of intensity and excitement, both of which emerge from a deeper knowledge of yourself and your partner. Eventually, in the best relationships, lasting love is based on the pleasure of full openness to another person—without anxiety, uncertainty, or fear. It surrounds you with a feeling that is both calming and deeply satisfying. In fact, it touches you at your very center and gives you a special sense of the worth of life itself.

MYTH

Love conquers all.

You need to reject this myth because it takes a lot more than loving feelings to deal with the problems inherent in building a life together. Depending on love to sustain your relationship misses a crucial point. Life is not one beautiful sunset after another. Life includes some beautiful sunsets, some gray days, and some full-blown storms. You need a more solid basis for your love—one that gives you a better chance of enjoying the sunsets and weathering the storms.

§

MYTH

We have a special love that will always bind us together.

While deep loving feelings can create a strong bond, it's unrealistic to expect love to last unless it's supported by your daily ways of relating to each other. A strong love is a great beginning, but building a life together takes a lot more than being in love. It takes compassion, understanding, compromise, communication, and creativity. Joint decisions have to be made about money, children, relatives, sex, time, and work. Values come into play that weren't considered at all in the decision to marry.

§

MYTH

We were meant for each other.

It's great to feel you've found the "right" partner, but it's shortsighted to think that's all it takes. As childhood sweethearts who had known each other all our lives, we certainly felt that we were meant for each other. But realistically, there is no such thing as only one Mr. or Ms. Right in the whole wide world. Certainly, it helps to feel you're starting off with the right person for you, but people change throughout their lives, so the right start only makes it possible to make your love stay; it's no guarantee.

❧

We can't live without each other.

Grand passion certainly has its place, but lasting love requires a great deal more. You need a relationship that's based on caring, commitment, respect, a sense of fairness, and a generally loving attitude toward your partner. Achieving this kind of relationship goes far beyond simply being in love. In fact, the idea that you can't live without each other reflects a certain desperateness about the relationship that is likely to sabotage its strength and vitality. This attitude causes any problem in the relationship to be seen as a life-or-death matter. Since all relationships have problems, this sets you up for a life of high anxiety.

❦

MYTH

Love just happens;
you either feel it or you don't.

No, love is not magic. It can feel magical when things are going right. But love is actually the by-product of all the attitudes and behaviors each of you brings to the relationship. Holding on to the idea that love exists in a vacuum only reinforces the false notion that the magical feeling of the first flush of new love is synonymous with love in its full, lasting richness (the kind that provides you a firm place to stand in the world).

So why should you reject these myths? Because they bring you to a love relationship with very unrealistic expectations. Conflicts and misunderstandings are probably inevitable as you struggle to cope with a world you never imagined. Initially, new love keeps these in the background, but it won't do so indefinitely. As the initial passion of new love burns lower, the nitty-gritty issues of building a life with another person move into the foreground—and reality hits you like a boulder. By rejecting these myths you can be prepared to deal effectively with life's daily issues as they arise instead of being shocked and discouraged by their presence. So the idea isn't to avoid problems (which is impossible), it's to deal with them in a way that strengthens your relationship instead of weakening it.

Both of you must make a lifelong commitment to deal directly and constructively with the many issues involved in building a life together. Without such a commitment and without good coping skills, the anger, hurt, jealousy, and resentment that most partners collect from their unresolved issues gradually extinguish the love they believed would never die.

It need not be so. You do not have to join those who dissolve their relationships when they are unable to live together happily, and you do not have to resign yourself to a relationship that is increasingly lifeless. You can direct the course of your love in a positive way, but you first need to rethink some of your attitudes and assumptions about love.

This is not a simple matter for most of us. The very fact that our ideas about love are based on assumptions means that we never thought them through in the first place; we just accepted them at face value. Unfortunately, most of our attitudes are based on fantasy and on the myths we've just discussed. You really can't begin to direct the course of your love until you question your assumptions and modify them to reflect reality.

Actually, if you could overcome all anxiety about making love stay and simply think clearly about what determines whether or not this happens, you'd find that deep down you already know these things. So we're not telling you anything new here. In a sense, we're giving you a blinding glimpse of the obvious. You're sure to have a sense of "aha, I knew that" as we identify the key insights involved in making love stay. Like many of the ideas in this book, they're things you have probably known at some point on some level, but you just forgot. So here's a reminder:

> 🐚 **The way you view love—what you believe to be true about love—can have a determining effect on the course of love in your life.**

You entered your current relationship (or you will enter one) with a complex set of attitudes and habits regarding what love is about and the proper ways of showing your love. You learned them from the people who raised you, people you've observed, things you've read, movies you've seen, and people with whom you've had loving relationships. The same is true for your partner. Some of your beliefs and preferences are similar to your partner's and some are different, but when viewed as a whole *each of you has a unique way of being in love.*

It's not a question of who's right and who's wrong. No one ever has all the right answers. What's important is a willingness to look honestly at what you've already learned about love, a conscious effort to retain the good and throw out the bad, and a willingness to continue learning what works best for the two of you.

For instance, one of you may think, "Love means never having to say you're sorry," while the other thinks, "Love means being willing to apologize for hurts and oversights, even if they're unintentional." One of you may think, "The primary way of expressing love is through words, saying, 'I love you' often," while the other thinks, "The primary way of expressing love is through actions: showing love by doing loving things." One of you may think, "Love means spending a great deal of time together," while the other thinks, "Love means being in each other's thoughts, not necessarily in their presence."

It's disquieting to acknowledge that your views of love can be so different from your partner's, that some of your most cherished beliefs about love aren't valid, and that the absolute security promised by true love isn't really possible. The whole idea of security is actually a negative one; it reinforces feelings of fear and anxiety based on needing constant reassurance. It also takes you out of being "in the flow" of whatever is really happening in your relationship.

It's futile to try to hold on to some static condition while life is moving right along. It's very much like the old proverb about entering a running stream: "You can never step in the same water twice." By trying to hold on to security, you're holding back the exciting growth in your relationship that's not only beneficial but essential if it's to last. As you and your partner increase your ability to care for each other and your relationship, you'll recognize that whatever discomfort you feel at discarding your attachment to security will recede into the background. You'll see that you're not really giving up anything that was real in the first place; you're simply getting rid of excess baggage that interferes with lasting love.

❧ Making love stay is a more complex undertaking than it first appears or than you were led to believe.

Popular songs tell us that true love overcomes everything and that it lasts forever. It ain't necessarily so. The danger in believing that true love has an omnipotent quality is that you may sit back and fail to do the ordinary day-to-day things that are needed to sustain love. A love relationship does not have a life of its own; it has the life you and your partner give it.

While this is a complex undertaking, it's quite manageable when broken down into the specific actions you need to take to sustain the quality of your love. Those actions are detailed in the individual entries that form the core of this book. The entire book is made up of simple, straightforward actions you can take to make your love stay.

This is the best news of all: the actions we're suggesting are within the capabilities of virtually everyone. Viewed one at a time, they are simple and easy to do. That doesn't mean you can simply memorize these suggestions and go through the motions of doing them. The actions will only be effective if they are part of a pattern and if they are performed with genuine caring, understanding, and sensitivity.

Most of us can sense whether our partner is being real or just acting in whatever way they think we want them to act. A superficial effort to do and say the "right" things without first getting your heart in the right place is likely to backfire. As the comedian George Carlin says in one of his routines, "You gotta wanna…" It's not enough to begrudgingly do these things; you've got to *want* to do them by virtue of understanding their importance and their benefit—if you're really serious about making love stay.

So as you go through the book, you'll notice that ideas on any given issue appear in many different places. While we've organized the items according to general themes, the same theme shows up in many places. For instance, early in the book we talk about a basic issue for most couples: finding a workable balance between needs for commitment and freedom. A little further on, in focusing on time and the need to respect individual needs for time alone, we point out how some people are suspicious of their partner's commitment if they spend much time apart. And still later on, in discussing feelings of jealousy, we describe the way possessiveness can feel like an infringement on a person's freedom. So no one page says all there is to say about a given issue. Each entry is like a small snapshot; taken all together they form the bigger picture of what's involved in making love stay.

❧ The structure of modern society and the fast pace of modern life don't naturally support love relationships.

You may feel that work absorbs a disproportionate amount of your time, attention, and energy, leaving too little of these precious resources for love relationships. Many of you are no doubt living in circumstances where you don't know your immediate neighbors, and the community support for marriage and family which existed for many of your parents is noticeably missing.

The sheer complexity of life today forces you to make more decisions about how to live than previous generations did. But the key to effectively dealing with these outside forces is to see yourselves as a couple, facing these pressures together. The pressures don't have to place a wedge between you; they can, in fact, strengthen your bond. For instance, we're fond of reminding each other whenever the going gets tough that "it's you and me against the world."

So the daily battles of life can be more easily fought when you're clear about where you stand in your relationship. Placing a high premium on the condition of your love doesn't mean not functioning in other areas of your life. Instead, it means having a safe, nurturing place (like a port in a storm) to go to.

We hope you're getting a clear sense that the ultimate payoff of working to make love stay is much greater than just the quality of your relationship. It affects the way you relate to the world at large. Lasting love tends to broaden your focus instead of restricting you, allowing you to function more effectively in all areas of your life. As we mentioned earlier, it gives you a special strength from which to face the world at large.

> **❧ The likelihood of sustaining love in a relationship is much greater when you both participate.**

In our society, women have traditionally been expected to take care of relationships. As long as women accept this as their role, there's little incentive for men to do their part. Unfortunately, this creates a lot of misunderstanding. A woman may get pretty discouraged at the condition of the relationship if she feels she's the only one trying to sustain its quality. And a man whose partner is assuming this responsibility may think there's no problem with the relationship as long as she's taking care of it. Meanwhile, the relationship is going downhill fast.

Both you and your partner need to be responsible for the life you're creating together. It is not sufficient to leave it to either one alone. If you're the only one attending to your relationship, you can't force your partner to participate; you can only encourage them by continually improving your own loving skills. But you also can't expect that your partner will automatically reciprocate just because you are committed to relating in a loving way. You can wait a very long time if you assume they'll eventually respond to your one-sided effort to have a good relationship.

This book can be the vehicle that allows you to end the standoff and clarify what's important to each of you—then concentrate on those specific things. It's a lot easier to focus on a few key issues one at a time than to tackle the whole big issue of "the condition of our relationship." You can't get by with a once-a-year report like the State of the Union Address. You need to have an ongoing sense of how your relationship is going so it doesn't get so far off track that it feels impossible to get it back on again.

> ❧ **Doing something positive each day to enhance your love relationship is more effective than a promise to love your partner forever.**

There is a proper place for exchanging formal vows such as those in a public wedding for those who choose to do it, and periodically renewing such vows can also be helpful, but putting a promise in writing and reciting it in public are not enough to make love stay. That's like buying a beautiful plant and never watering it. It may have cost a good bit and you may profess to value it. You may even have every intention of taking care of it. But you're busy, you're distracted by other things—and you still see the plant through the image in your mind's eye of its initial beauty when you bought it. Meanwhile, it's gradually losing its vitality—and if you wait too long to notice what's happening, it may be too late.

Love is not so different from a plant in that it too needs nourishment and ongoing attention in order to grow. Consciously doing loving things in a timely way is essential to making love stay. This kind of attention doesn't have to take a lot of time, a lot of money, or a lot of energy. It can be as quick as a smile or a kiss hello. It can be as inexpensive as the gift of caring demonstrated by an unexpected offer to run an errand or make a phone call. It can be as simple as sitting together watching a sunset or watching your children at play.

You can open this book to almost any page and get a sense of something you can do to enrich your love. Most of the ideas arise out of a loving attitude. It's not so much the specific act as the attitude with which you do it that keeps your love alive. Love can't be frozen in time and put on the shelf. So enjoy the memory of whatever initial vows or promises you made to each other, but remember that was only the beginning—not the be-all, end-all of your love.

The Payoff Is Well Worth the Effort

If you have some resistance to working to make your love stay, it may be based on feeling that love should be effortless—not something you have to work at. But it's really not work in the way we usually think of work. Actually, it can be a tremendous source of energy, joy, and satisfaction, but only if you reframe the way you think about work and love—and only if you reorder your priorities to give love the place it deserves.

Yes, it takes time and energy, but once you get a sense of the incredible payoff for your effort, you won't be able to imagine living any other way. It's a little like the experience you may have had with exercise. If you start by seeing exercise only as something you ought to do, you're likely to dread the time and energy it takes. Many people never get past their negative attitude toward exercise to experience the true benefits. If you're a person who values fitness and knows from firsthand experience the benefits of exercise, you know that the positive results outweigh the time and energy it takes—and whatever resistance you may have had gives way to wanting to do it.

Of course, just as you need to start with an exercise you enjoy, you need to start with a person you genuinely love. It figures that you can't make love stay if you don't start with a real love in the first place. But assuming you start with the raw material, you're ready to build on that beginning. That's what this book aims to help you do.

Reading sections of *Making Love Stay* aloud with your partner and discussing your reactions can provide a way to talk about some issues that you may not have found a way to address previously. This can also enable you to nip some problems in the bud and avoid others altogether. Above all, use these ideas in a positive way—to find better ways of relating to your partner, not to show them their attitudes or behaviors are wrong.

This book can be used in several other ways, according to your mood at the moment and your goal. You can use it as a handbook, picking it up and reading it at any point and referring to it at random. You're likely to discover ideas that you had forgotten or lost sight of and be reminded to focus on them again.

Or you can use it as a reference, going directly to whatever points you see as most relevant to your current (or past) relationship. But of course no issue exists in isolation; everything is connected to everything else.

Or you can read it all the way through from front to back to get an overall perspective. In fact, you'll miss a great deal of the benefit of the book if you don't do this at some point.

Each of the book's seven chapters addresses one of the steps involved in the process of making love stay. Although this process varies from one couple to the next, there are fundamental stages that apply to everyone, and the order in which you work on them is important. So we've organized the book in a way that reflects that order.

This first chapter has discussed the nature of love and its place in your life. In chapter 2 we will show you the path to making love stay—which happens to be honest communication. Chapter 3 addresses the core issues that lie beneath the day-to-day stresses, strains, and joys of your relationship. In chapter 4, we discuss the nitty-gritty issues of daily living that stimulate most of the differences you will face as a couple. Then in chapter 5 we talk about ways to handle the negative reactions to your differences. Chapter 6 describes the actions you can take to sustain your love. And the last chapter reinforces what you've learned by showing you the benefits of following this path.

So we're taking you step by step through the process of making your love stronger and better with every passing day. By the time you're finished, you'll have a realistic perception of lasting love and some tools to help you achieve it. But of course we can only make suggestions; it's up to you and your partner to make it happen.

In the final analysis, the most important insight we have to offer is that making love stay is a never-ending process. That may seem like bad news, but it's not. After all these years, we still practice the principles discussed in this book, and it's not a chore. The work of love is an exciting, enlivening activity that not only allows you to feel good about yourself and your relationship, but also provides a special source of strength and confidence from which to face the world. So if you're tired of messing around with superficial quick fixes and are ready to make some dramatic changes in the way you relate, then you're in for an exciting time.

2

Committing to Honest Communication

The Path to Making Love Stay

*Y*ou and your partner may have very different views on the role of communication in your relationship. The classic complaint from many wives is "He won't talk" and from husbands, "She talks constantly." According to Deborah Tannen, a keen observer of the differences between male and female communication styles and the author of *You Just Don't Understand,* a woman tends to think the relationship is working as long as she and her partner are talking about it, and a man tends to think the relationship is *not* working if they have to talk about it. Simply recognizing this difference in perceptions can be the first step toward finding a reasonable balance—talking enough so that each of you understands how the other feels about your relationship without "talking it to death."

It helps to reflect on how our ways of viewing communication got polarized in the first place. We didn't invent these differences; they've been around for years. You can no doubt recall examples in your own family of how generations repeat the same pattern. We have some vivid examples from our family.

Visiting Grandmother Vaughan's on Sunday was a family ritual. She lived in a big old farm house set back from the road, with a wraparound porch and a swing. The driveway leading up to the house was fairly long, and there was a clear view from the house of any car entering the driveway. Invariably, as we approached the house, we'd see Uncle George sitting in the swing—and Uncle George always saw us too. As soon as we came into view, he began moving out of the swing, down the steps, and along the side of the house toward the barn. By the time we pulled up to the house and got out of the car, he would be rounding the back of the house and then move out of sight. It wasn't that Uncle George disliked us. He simply didn't care for talking, so he just removed himself from the talking scene. (He *would* show up for the noon meal and sit silently at the table while the talking continued, then it was back to the barn.)

Uncle George was not unique. Other males in the family found various ways to avoid talking. James's dad routinely took a nap after lunch in the same room where the women were chattering nonstop, thoroughly enjoying the chance to catch up on the happenings in the family since their last gathering.

This may sound like men never talk, which, of course, is not true. It's just that men and women prefer to talk about different things and at different times, and "relationship talk" is stereotypically considered "women's talk." Realistically, however, it takes two to make a relationship, and two to talk about it. This doesn't mean that either men or women have to totally adopt the other's style. It just means that you need to find some balance between your preferences about the *amount* of talk so you can focus on the *kind* of talk you need.

Since neither of you is likely to be a very good mind reader, you will in essence be strangers to each other if you don't learn to talk about the really important stuff of life—your individual wants, needs, hopes, joys, and fears.

You probably have your own sense of the importance of good communication in your relationship. We believe it's hard to overstate. It allows you to know each other at deeper and deeper levels, providing the basis for trust and a willingness to be vulnerable. It's also essential to working through the issues that usually interfere with making love stay.

Communication is necessary not only to solve problems, but also to share the joys of life. You need to talk about all your feelings, good and bad, expressing those of love as well as those of irritation. You probably have both kinds of feelings more than you think, but you may let the irritation block out the expressions of love. Naturally, communication is going to seem like a problem when it's used only to express negative feelings.

We've found that when there's a block in our communication, what suffers most is the good stuff. If we leave an interaction with unresolved feelings, they carry over and stifle our willingness to say anything positive that might come to mind. After missing out on some really good experiences, we've finally learned to break through that resistance and say the positive things we feel. The loss represented by the unspoken kind word is greater than you might think; you lose part of the glue that binds you together.

Another thing that might interfere with your efforts to communicate effectively is the idea that you have to learn some special techniques. While some general insights about communication can be helpful, many of the formal techniques feel rigid and artificial. For instance, a popular technique designed to let your partner know that you heard and understood what they said is to say, "What I hear you saying is..." Well, we tried that technique and learned that for us it didn't work. Not only did it not feel reassuring, it felt gimmicky and patronizing—not at all genuine.

Rest assured, you don't have to learn a new way of speaking in order to improve your communication. What's important is to get your heart in the right place. That means being absolutely honest with yourself about your motives for talking. Are you talking in order to sustain, build, and improve your relationship? Or are you talking as a way of criticizing, complaining, and proving you're right? Your attitude makes all the difference. So while techniques can be helpful (and we're offering some ideas along that line), they won't do any good unless they're used in the right spirit.

You know from your own experience that even the smoothest talker isn't effective if you feel deep down that they're not honest or sincere. We all tend to hear the feelings behind the words, regardless of the particular words that are used. For instance, when a clerk completes your transaction by repeating the words "Have a nice day" in a monotone with no eye contact or human connection, do you really think they care whether you have a nice day? It's clear that words are a very small part of any message; the motives are what really count. So if your clear intention is to use communication as a path to making love stay, you're likely to be successful—regardless of your technical skills.

All this talk about communication may not seem critical to you if you think you already communicate pretty well. That's great—*if* you're dealing openly and thoroughly with all kinds of issues. Smooth communication *can* be a problem if it's only smooth because you never deal with difficult problems. Having a lot of communication doesn't necessarily mean it's good communication. We've known couples who keep their communication at such a superficial level that they only talk about mundane things and never discuss differences or deep feelings. All too often the most critical issues are the ones that don't get discussed.

As we mentioned in the first chapter, this is what happened to us. We thought we were pretty good at communicating until we faced a real crisis (James's extramarital affairs). We literally spent thousands of hours trying to understand and deal with what had happened. This forced us to take a good, hard look at all the issues we had avoided discussing. We had withheld so many of our thoughts and feelings through the years that it was quite an ordeal to work through all the "stuff" that had built up between us. We committed ourselves to honest communication—breaking our old patterns of relating and establishing new ones.

Based on our experience, we strongly suggest that whatever you most stubbornly resist talking about is likely to be precisely what you most need to talk about—before you hit a crisis like ours. Maybe you think you already know each other so well that you're not vulnerable to any surprises like this. That's what we thought. Since we had grown up together and had been childhood sweethearts, we thought we knew all about each other. What we failed to do was consider how dramatically people can change through the years and that you don't continue to know someone unless you honestly discuss your changes with each other.

You can't really know each other unless you establish and maintain a strong commitment to honesty. Good communication is synonymous with honest, complete communication. Don't let the idea of honesty scare you off; it doesn't mean dumping your negative feelings on your partner. The key is responsible honesty, which we'll explain in more detail in this chapter.

This chapter will also help clarify the process of developing honest communication as a couple. You'll learn that honesty is more than just not lying; it's also not withholding relevant information from your partner. And you'll learn why this kind of honesty is so essential. You'll also be able to recognize what you've been doing that's ineffective, as well as getting a sense of the important role that listening plays in good communication.

Most of the entries are aimed at strengthening your bond by strengthening your ability to talk to each other in ways that reinforce your loving feelings. Many of the good things in life and in love are the result of honest communication. As you incorporate these ideas into your interactions with each other, you'll see what a positive difference they can make in the quality of your relationship.

MAKING A JOINT COMMITMENT

The most important ingredient in sustaining a solid, loving relationship is a commitment to honest communication.

- ❧ It allows you to know each other at a level of intimacy that leads to a deeper, more lasting trust than usually exists.
- ❧ It allows your relationship to change and keep pace with the changes that inevitably occur in each of you separately.
- ❧ It keeps the channels of communication clear by continuously providing challenges that can be used for growth.
- ❧ It allows each of you to know yourself at ever deeper levels.

You may consider yourself honest as long as you don't tell an outright lie. You may feel you're still being honest when you simply withhold information you aren't asked about directly. But honest communication goes beyond being truthful in what you say; it also means volunteering all thoughts and feelings that are relevant to the relationship.

You may be tempted to think it's OK to tell little white lies or to withhold information out of fear of hurting your partner. Don't rationalize your unwillingness to devote the time and energy necessary to deal with the complexity of honest communication. Just do it!

Commit to talking in an honest and forthright way.

MAKING A JOINT COMMITMENT

Think of honesty in its broadest terms as a means of building trust. It includes a lot more than what you say to your partner in words. You need to be honest in your actions and your reactions—in the total way you present yourself.

It's easy to be honest when you're confident your partner will respond favorably to your words and actions. It's difficult when you're not sure how they will react or when you believe they will disapprove. You can realistically expect some disapproval and some disagreement with consistently honest expression. It's inevitable since no two people have identical perceptions, attitudes, values, and preferences in life.

Never waver in your commitment to honesty. It will see you through the differences that are common to all relationships, and it will provide the basis for lasting trust.

Pursue honesty as the single greatest
tool for building trust.

MAKING A JOINT COMMITMENT

Communication is not just a matter of talking more; it's a matter of talking about the right things—and in the right way. It involves accurately identifying the problems you face as a couple and effectively dealing with them on an ongoing basis.

You can see the results of a lack of honest communication by simply observing couples in a restaurant. Those who aren't talking are almost always those who have been together for quite some time and who have suppressed so many of their true emotions (both positive and negative) that they have become strangers to each other. They feel safer saying nothing. This kind of lifeless relationship is all too common.

Too often, you fail to talk about your feelings. It takes a tremendous amount of energy to keep them buried, and as they accumulate, you lose the vitality of your relationship. But you can recapture this energy and put it to productive use in working through these feelings and making love stay.

Agree to share your thoughts and
feelings on an ongoing basis.

UNLEARNING INEFFECTIVE
COMMUNICATION HABITS

Whenever there's a discrepancy between what you say and what you do, your partner is more likely to believe your actions than your words. You know this to be true from your own experience. When you're involved in an important verbal exchange, you carefully observe the facial expressions of the other person to see if their expressions match their words.

If you want to communicate clearly, it's crucial that your eyes and facial expressions reinforce your words. When there's a difference between what you say and how you look, your partner will be more affected by the look than by the words. Frowns, looks of irritation or impatience, and lack of eye contact are some of the common ways of undermining confidence in your positive words.

Use these understandings to keep your communications clean and to give them maximum impact.

Remember that what you do speaks
louder than what you say.

UNLEARNING INEFFECTIVE
COMMUNICATION HABITS

Words do make a difference. Part of being a responsible adult involves (1) understanding that words do hurt and (2) making a conscious effort to be accurate and considerate in the words you use.

Don't let your anger cause you to say things you'll later regret. A five-year-old can be forgiven for shouting at a parent, "I hate you!" They haven't yet learned how to accurately convey their feelings. What they really mean is, "I hate what you just did."

A teenager can be forgiven for whining, "You never let me stay out as late as my friends." Even when a parent knows it to be an inaccurate statement, it's easy to overlook because most of us can still remember how the world looks to a teenager.

As adults, we need to have different expectations of ourselves. We know that words hurt. It follows that we should avoid loaded, judgmental words that are likely to clog up the communication channels.

Be considerate in your choice of words.

LEARNING NEW SKILLS—
CONTINUOUSLY

You can always improve your communication skills, regardless of your current abilities. Your most powerful tool in developing better communication skills is your genuine desire to do so. With the right attitude, you can learn to be a good communicator. Good communication includes:

- Using "I" statements (to describe how you feel) rather than "you" statements (which blame your partner for your feelings).
- Sharing your observations and checking them out rather than making assumptions about your partner's words or actions.
- Speaking in terms of differing opinions, not in terms of absolute right and wrong.
- Focusing on describing your partner's behavior, not judging them as a person.
- Sharing ideas and information rather than giving advice.

Work on your communication skills.

LEARNING NEW SKILLS—
CONTINUOUSLY

You know how good it feels to be truly heard and accepted, and how bad it feels to be ignored or rejected. None of us is born a good listener, but we can all learn to become one. Some key skills in good listening include:

- Making yourself available when the other person needs to talk, not just when it's convenient for you.
- Setting aside your personal agenda so that you can be fully present for what the other wants to say.
- Withholding judgment. (You don't have to agree with what's being said, but you need to accept it in order to support your partner's ability to talk freely.)
- Consciously avoiding the knee-jerk reaction to give advice or offer solutions to problems the other may be describing.

- Responding both nonverbally (for example, by nodding your head or smiling) and with short verbal acknowledgments to show you're hearing and understanding what they're saying.
- Maintaining eye contact and touching when appropriate to show support and attention.
- Listening to the feelings behind the words and accepting them. (Sometimes they're more important than the words themselves.)
- Listening to what is not said. An omission can be a revealing clue to the overall message.

Be a good listener.

MAKING TIME TO TALK

You can prevent a lot of problems through regular, in-depth communication about issues that are important to both of you. It's easy to get caught up in daily activities and avoid taking the time to talk about your ongoing attitudes and feelings. But you can save a lot of time in the long run by anticipating and resolving issues before they become full-blown crises.

Regular communication is even more valuable as a means of staying in touch with each other—thereby enjoying the intimacy that comes from this kind of close connection.

Set aside time for communicating;
don't wait for a crisis.

DISCLOSING

Go beyond a superficial knowing of each other by constantly sharing more fully just who you are as a person. Closeness comes from a deeper knowing—which results from a willingness to expose your private thoughts, hopes, dreams, and fears.

You may be afraid of such vulnerability, but there's strength in developing the kind of closeness that comes only through a deep knowing of each other. You deserve to be loved for who you are—not for some artificial image you project. If and when the truth behind the image is exposed, there may be no basis for continuing what was a false connection. In the final analysis, it's safer to be known (and loved) for who you really are.

Strengthen your bond by getting to know
each other at ever deeper levels

DISCLOSING

You're a different person today than you were five years ago, and five years from now you will have changed in still more ways—ways that even you can't predict right now. Don't expect your partner to be a mind reader. To keep your trust strong and growing, you need to keep them informed about your changing attitudes and beliefs, some of which may be subtle and difficult to discern.

Be willing to disclose yourself in this way—and invite your partner to do the same. Even though there may not be total enthusiasm for everything you share, expressing whatever changes you're feeling will help you clarify what's really happening. And it's the only way to stay in touch with each other on an ongoing basis.

Renew your trust by continually
disclosing yourself.

EXPRESSING FEELINGS/EMOTIONS

Laugh together.

Cry together.

Develop a full relationship; be a whole person with your partner. Take the risk of disclosing your greatest hopes and your deepest fears. It's frightening, but it's part of developing trust and intimacy.

Make it easy for your partner to express their feelings without fear of being judged or categorized in any way. Don't underestimate the difficulty of this. Men in particular have been conditioned to hide their softer, gentler feelings. Women have been conditioned to hide their angry, controlling feelings. And both sexes fail to fully express their light, joyous feelings. This is a major problem since love thrives on the free expression of feelings.

Accept and share your full range of emotions.

EXPRESSING FEELINGS/EMOTIONS

No matter how much you and your partner care for each other, there will be times when you upset each other. Forgetting an anniversary, failing to call when you said you would, disclosing something your partner thought should remain private—these are some of the countless ways you disappoint each other even with the best of intentions.

It's important to deal consciously and constructively with these small disappointments. You certainly don't need to discuss each one as it occurs. Sometimes it's more effective to mention it later. But it's risky to think you never have to deal with them. This increases the likelihood that each of you will continue to disappoint the other and that you will accumulate resentments that will interfere with your normal expressions of love.

Be prepared to deal with problems in your relationship; they're unavoidable.

EXPRESSING FEELINGS/EMOTIONS

Trouble comes to everyone. Many relationships suffer because one or both partners haven't learned to face life's challenges with composure and balance. Take an honest look at your coping skills.

When you're extremely angry at something that happened in some other part of your life outside your relationship, are you likely to be short-tempered with your partner? When you're deeply troubled by a serious problem, do you typically withdraw from your partner—even though they have nothing to do with the problem?

Make a commitment today to continuously improve your coping skills so that neither your partner nor your relationship suffers unfairly from the problems that will surely come your way.

Don't shut yourself off from your partner
when trouble comes your way.

AFFIRMING

You may get so bogged down by the roles you play in the relationship that you lose sight of the person behind the role. This is especially true in long-lasting relationships that have experienced numerous problems and stresses.

Recovering the sense you had of your partner when you first met them may require more than just privately trying to remember those days. It will help if the two of you reminisce about your early time together—perhaps by looking at photos and discussing what attracted you to each other. Don't let those two loving people get buried under the strains that are a normal part of life.

Renew your love by reflecting on what attracted you in the first place.

AFFIRMING

Be gentle in your assessment of your partner. Study them; appreciate the little things that make them interesting and different from anyone else. Embrace their imperfections along with your own.

Show your partner that you think they're special. Tell them over and over. The need for affirmation that you're loved and cared for is never completely satisfied. It's not enough to have once been full of praise for your partner.

Self-esteem is very fragile and gets pounded by so many forces outside the relationship that it's all the more important to feel appreciated by the most significant person in your life.

Accept your partner completely;
appreciate their uniqueness.

AFFIRMING

No matter how much your partner achieves, no matter how self-confident they are, they still need to be acknowledged as a worthy person. Do it with touch and don't be shy about accepting their validation in return. Touch is unique in its power to affirm.

Use touch to validate your partner.

EXPRESSING LOVE

Find your own unique ways to express your love. Imitating others will work only if it feels right to you and your partner.

Follow your impulses whenever you feel a sudden surge of loving feelings. The spontaneous feelings of love that come at unexpected times can be very special—even more special than your carefully planned demonstrations of love.

Don't let these moments pass. Schedules and responsibilities may cause you to block these feelings, but if you waste these wonderful opportunities, you may not be able to re-create them later.

Loving feelings can be quite fleeting, and it's important to express them before they slip away.

*Be inventive and ingenious in
your expressions of love.*

EXPRESSING LOVE

While romantic gestures aren't sufficient to form the basis of your love, they are wonderful as reflections of your joy in being together and as a way of expressing your loving feelings.

Women, especially, are likely to long for a little romance in their long-term relationships. They often complain that men are not romantic enough—that they don't bring flowers, send love notes, or think of other little romantic touches. But romance, of course, is a two-way street. Many men appreciate *receiving* flowers or love notes.

Together, the two of you can experience romantic feelings by watching a beautiful sunset, walking in the moonlight, listening to romantic music, or reading love poems aloud.

> *Be a little romantic; this can add*
> *pleasure to a loving relationship.*

EXPRESSING LOVE

"I love you."

"You're a special person."

"I love the way you laugh."

"I love it when you get totally serious."

There are endless ways to profess your love verbally. Don't be shy about it. Use your own words to express your true feelings in a spontaneous way. It's unlikely you can overdo it as long as you're sincere and thoughtful in telling your partner how you feel.

It's not enough to simply assume your partner knows they're loved. They still need to hear the verbal message, "I love you." Your partner is not a mind reader. They may think you love them, but they *know* you love them when you show them and tell them so. Love grows and thrives on free expression.

Speak your love out loud.

EXPRESSING LOVE

"I like your smile."

"I love the way you take care of your body."

"I want to spend my life with you."

"I love you more with each passing year."

Verbal expressions of love are great, but so are written ones. In fact, the written word adds an extra dimension. It can be savored in a different way, in the first moment it's read—and later as well.

Putting some thoughts in writing whenever you're apart is a good habit to develop, but don't wait for those times. An unexpected love note when you're together can have an even greater impact.

Special occasions provide more good opportunities to express loving feelings. If you buy a card with a verse, add a note explaining why you chose it. Better still, buy a blank card and write your own message. It doesn't need to be a poem, just sincere words describing the way you feel about your partner. Some of these will be saved and cherished for many years and will continue to add to the loving feelings that flow back and forth.

Put your love in writing

EXPRESSING LOVE

Look lovingly into your partner's eyes. Eye contact is one of the most effective tools you have to communicate your feelings. Don't underestimate the power of openly showing your love with your eyes and facial expressions.

Even when there are no words, you communicate volumes with your looks alone. The simple things—a smile, a wink, a look of being interested or concerned or just connected—make a tremendous difference in your overall communication.

Show your love in your eyes.

EXPRESSING LOVE

Touch is quite possibly the most reliable and the most powerful means you have of expressing your love. Words can be misunderstood or misinterpreted because their meaning depends on so many other things, such as facial expression, tone of voice, previous word associations, and so forth.

Touch, by comparison, is straightforward and relatively unmistakable. Use it freely to reinforce and augment your verbal expressions of love.

Expressing your love through touch says:

"I care about you."

"I'm here for you."

"You're important in my life."

Touch creates a sense of comfort and belonging, of having someone on your side, of being bonded together in a fundamental way.

There are times when no words are sufficient to convey your caring and concern for your partner. It's at these times that touch is even more critical as a means of communicating your love.

Express your love through touch.

TOUCHING

Touch your partner every day, not just in times of crisis. Chances are you respond instinctively with loving touch when your partner is in any sort of distress. At such times their need for comfort is obvious. What's not so obvious is the need we all have for loving touch on a continual basis.

Infants literally must have touch in order to survive and grow. As an adult, you can survive without it, but a daily dose of loving touch makes a definite contribution to your mental and physical health and your sense of well-being. Don't permit busy agendas to crowd out the touch you and your partner need to live fully.

Consciously touch as a means of
promoting wellness.

TOUCHING

In an ideal world, your partner would always anticipate your needs for touch and respond without your asking. In the real world, it's essential that you initiate and ask for the touch you need and want. You might try imitating your cat or dog. They do it unashamedly every day.

Don't hesitate to ask for the touch you need.

TOUCHING

It's hard to overstate the benefits of good skin contact. Twenty minutes of loving, nude cuddling in the morning and evening will match any meditation program ever devised. In fact, it probably is a meditation program. "Ohmm" seems to come automatically with loving skin contact.

If you think you can't afford 20 minutes, then make it two minutes or whatever time you can spare. A full hug with clothes on is good, but it's no substitute for skin-on-skin.

Make time for skin-on-skin contact.

TOUCHING

Sleep in the nude. It's your best opportunity for a daily dose of good skin-on-skin. Clothes have their proper place, but it's not in bed. Modesty has its place, but not when it interferes with your availability for the nourishment of skin contact.

Babies know what's important. They aren't the least bit self-conscious about their bodies, and they love nude contact. You were that way as an infant. You can recapture that innocence now, and it will enhance your love every day of your life.

Sleep naked—all the time.

TOUCHING

The child in you and your partner still loves to be held and caressed even though you're grown-ups and may find it awkward to crawl into each other's laps. Never mind the feelings of awkwardness. Do it anyway.

Hold your partner; caress them

TOUCHING

Don't make the mistake of touching intimately only when you intend to have sex. If you're not in good contact outside the bedroom, you're unlikely to be close inside the bedroom.

This nonsexual touch can be especially meaningful because it implies a kind of caring for the total person that goes beyond physical attraction. Your touch can be as simple as a hand on the shoulder or as extensive as a back rub or a full-body massage.

And you don't have to curtail all touch when you step outside your house. Of course, you don't want to make a spectacle of yourselves in public, but holding hands or touching in other supportive ways maintains your feelings of closeness and connectedness as you move out into the world.

Do not restrict your loving touch to the bedroom

TOUCHING

There's no place in a loving relationship for any kind of touch except loving touch. You may have grown up in a family where hitting, pushing, and restraining were frequently used to express anger and feelings of disapproval. You may even have accepted that this is what loving parents have to do when they're raising children who can't or won't listen to reason.

Don't kid yourself. You're a grown-up and your partner is a grown-up. Negative touch may relieve your anger or frustration momentarily, but it will not help your relationship. Quite the contrary, it will diminish your relationship. You may not notice it immediately, but sooner or later, the effects will show up.

Make sure your touch consistently
communicates love and caring.

3

The Core Issues Beneath the Surface

$\mathcal{W}$e spent much of our lives together rehashing our differences about the issues that dominate the discussions of most couples: money, sex, time, kids, work, friends, relatives, and the countless mundane maintenance issues that go with daily living. After years of this, we began to notice that the same arguments would crop up when we were discussing different issues. We finally realized that whatever the particular topic, it usually only represented some deeper issue beneath the surface.

For instance, we found that most of our differences about the kids weren't really about the kids at all; the real issue between us was one of control. Each of us wanted the kids to be raised in accordance with our own individual ideas and opinions. Control was the core issue that lay beneath the surface.

Likewise, we found that most of our disagreements about use of time or about mundane chores weren't really about those issues either. The real issue between us was one of fairness. Each of us judged the degree to which the other was thoughtful in their use of time and the degree to which the other was doing their fair share of the daily maintenance work—and we made our individual assessments of whether the other was being fair.

When having conflicts, it certainly helps if you're able to identify what the real issues are—and this isn't always obvious. So we're devoting this chapter to identifying some of these core issues: commitment/ freedom, values/expectations, power/control, competition/cooperation, respect/self-esteem, and fairness/equality.

After getting a clearer sense of how these core issues are reflected in your daily interactions, you'll be better prepared to deal with the nitty-gritty issues we'll discuss in chapter 4. In many ways, the problems you have as a couple in dealing with the daily issues (like sex, money, and kids) are just symptoms of the deeper problems, and you won't be able to effectively deal with them until you get clear about what lies underneath them.

Because we've worked a lot on this dilemma in our own relationship, we can now almost immediately recognize the core issue represented by a particular problem. We also see that the core issue may be different for each of us in a particular situation. For instance, both of us have always played tennis. We grew up together and played for the same high-school team. Each of us was the number one player for our team. But through the years, things changed. James continued to pursue tennis seriously, but I didn't care for competition and felt too much time constraint to go out and play just for the enjoyment of it.

After the birth of our children, my free time was even more restricted and James continued to play as much as before—even competing in a tournament while I was taken to the hospital to give birth. (Fortunately, he finished the match and got to the hospital before the baby came.)

For many years, we focused only on the issue of time spent playing tennis—as if that were the problem. We finally recognized that there were issues underlying this problem that we should be focusing on instead. We discovered that these issues were somewhat different for each of us; the core issue for James was freedom while the core issue for me was fairness and respect. And core issues for both of us were differences in needs and expectations. We could have talked all day every day about time spent playing tennis and it wouldn't have done any good—because time wasn't the real issue.

To use another example, our issues regarding money actually reflect differences in values and life-style preferences. To this day, we can both look at the same financial figures and assess them in totally different ways. James is much more optimistic and materially oriented while I take a negative view of most money matters and prefer a more basic life-style. This is a problem that continues to take up a lot of our time. We're committed to living our lives together—but it isn't always easy when we are so diametrically opposed in many of our preferences about life-style.

We certainly haven't resolved all our differences about core issues. In fact, resolving these differences is not a reasonable goal. The real task is to understand what they are and continually remind ourselves (and each other) that there is no one right way. Each of us is justified in having our own preferences, and we've come to respect the legitimacy of our different ways of seeing things. In fact, we feel we've benefitted by having to accommodate our differences instead of going overboard in our respective directions.

Nowhere is this kind of balance and compromise more beneficial than in the area of dealing with our kids. Even now that they're grown, we're philosophically in tune while still having differences based on issues related to commitment and generosity of spirit. My commitment and supportiveness of the kids is greater than what James thinks is best for everyone involved. And James's tendency toward standard parental attitudes (thinking he knows best) bothers my sense of respect for the kids and my desire to treat them with equality. The positive result of our differences is that the kids get the benefit of both kinds of parenting—and both are needed and effective at different times and in different circumstances.

Not only do the kids benefit from these differences, but our relationship benefits as well. If we agreed on all the core issues, we wouldn't spend time and energy discussing them—and we wouldn't know each other as well or as deeply as we do by virtue of these serious conversations. This, in turn, brings us closer and strengthens our bond—making our love grow stronger.

Here are a few more personal examples to help you in identifying your own core issues:

Most of our work issues reflect deeper issues of power and control, equality and self-esteem. My eight years as a full-time homemaker with small children afforded me less status than James derived from his Ph.D. This imbalance continues to be somewhat of a problem, and even with my subsequent success as a consultant, a speaker, and an author , I still find myself dealing with the core issues of respect and self-esteem. Work has never been the primary avenue through which I judge my self-worth—but it's nevertheless an issue for me because society tends to judge people that way.

It was easier for us to see that maintenance issues (all those mundane chores that turn the wheels of daily life) were rooted in something more basic—like equality and mutual respect. By focusing on these core issues, we found it much easier to deal in a practical, nonemotional way with who does the cleaning, the cooking, the shopping, and the bill paying.

This way of understanding problems allows you to get beneath the surface and deal with the basic values that are at the heart of your differences. We now see that none of the issues we originally thought of as problems were actually the problem. Now we don't get distracted by issues like money, time, or kids; we know they represent deeper issues like fairness, control, and commitment.

We hope that when problems arise in your own relationship, you'll use these personal examples to help you determine the more critical underlying issues they represent for you. Reading and discussing the entries in this chapter can also enable you to identify which core issues are underneath your own daily disagreements.

It's critical to deal with these deeper issues. Since they dictate most of our attitudes about ourselves, our partner, and our relationship, they often make or break a relationship. If they aren't dealt with, they can fester and cause ongoing resentment and hostility that will kill your loving feelings. But getting a handle on them will allow each of you to accept and respect the other in a way that enhances your love.

COMMITMENT/FREEDOM

To give your best in a relationship and to get the greatest benefit from your commitment, the commitment needs to be freely chosen. Forcing it will only lead to negative consequences and will eventually diminish the relationship.

If you've chosen commitment, you already know some of the deep psychological and spiritual benefits to be gained from a loving relationship. But you may also have a strong desire for the freedom you feel you've lost by making this commitment.

This is one of the greatest paradoxes in life. Realistically, all of life involves trade-offs, and you need to constantly remind yourself that you must choose what is most important to you and be willing to forgo other desires that undermine that choice.

*Accept the paradoxes in life; commitment
is great, and so is freedom.*

COMMITMENT/FREEDOM

Since both commitment and freedom are seen as desirable, you may find that trying to balance your needs for both presents quite a dilemma. You value the sense of belonging that comes with commitment, but you also value having a degree of independent control over your life.

When you're in a committed relationship, you may tend to focus more on the drawbacks to commitment while fantasizing about the advantages of freedom. (Of course, if you were completely free, you would probably be more aware of the drawbacks to freedom and feel more desirous of the advantages of commitment.)

It's important to recognize that there is no perfect, permanent resolution to the dilemma posed by freedom and commitment. But you need to avoid getting so far out of balance that you overreact in an irresponsible way. You can reduce this risk by maintaining a sense of individuality within the context of being part of a couple. The following pages offer some ideas for doing this.

Maintain a good balance between satisfying your need for commitment and your need for freedom

COMMITMENT/FREEDOM

Give your partner the freedom they need. You may feel anxious about whether you can trust each other without significantly restricting your mutual freedom. Realistically, neither of you can control the other by denying their freedom to pursue individual interests.

In the final analysis, there are no guarantees, but when you support your partner's rights as an independent person, you increase the likelihood they will feel more comfortable with their commitment to the relationship

Realize that relationships always involve risk

COMMITMENT/FREEDOM

You may try to ignore your fears about individual freedom in your relationship. Don't pretend there are no risks in the hope they will go away. You can bury your concerns temporarily, but they won't stay buried. In fact, they may grow stronger. And they'll continue to surface and create misgivings about where things stand between you.

Talk about your fears with your partner, but keep them in perspective. Fear can be your friend when you take it as a cue that you need to change something you're doing, but don't allow it to overwhelm you.

Any persistent concern that you do not discuss creates feelings of distance between you. This gradually increases the likelihood that the two of you will avoid other problems as they arise—leading to a growing sense of alienation that makes it difficult to discuss any issue in a nonthreatening way.

Don't create additional strain in your relationship by allowing your fear of risks to immobilize you. Clear thinking will let you see that being a captive of your fears only increases the risks to your relationship.

Keep the risks of freedom in perspective by acknowledging them instead of trying to ignore them.

DEPENDENCE/
INDEPENDENCE/INTERDEPENDENCE

You were born totally dependent. When you were growing up, your parents were probably torn between their desire that you become more independent and concerns for your welfare that tended to keep you dependent. You may have received little or no training or encouragement to be interdependent—yet that is what's needed in developing a satisfying love relationship.

Interdependence involves a delicate balance between dependence and independence. It's like a seesaw where each of you is dependent on the other to hold up their side. (If both of you were on the same side of the seesaw, it wouldn't work; it takes separate efforts but a joint commitment to working together.) It involves giving *of* yourself without giving *up* yourself.

Interdependence involves moving out into the world as a separate person—but with a strong home base that's not forgotten. It means caring without clinging. In the final analysis, it means being a whole person while still being part of a couple.

Learn the fine art of being an interdependent partner.

DEPENDENCE/
INDEPENDENCE/INTERDEPENDENCE

It's good to have a strong commitment to maintain your relationship, but feeling that you can't live without your partner will almost certainly lead to problems.

Avoid the trap of believing you need the other to be complete or that you should think like your partner, have the same preferences, do everything together, and so forth. This doesn't mean you must erect barriers between each other, only that you need to allow for individual functioning.

If you are desperate and clinging, your love is likely to be seen as a burden. This dependent kind of behavior is very unappealing and does nothing to reinforce feelings of love.

> *Don't be completely dependent on
> your partner or on their love.*

DEPENDENCE/
INDEPENDENCE/INTERDEPENDENCE

No one—not even your partner—can make you happy over the long haul. First of all, no one else can fully know what it takes to make you happy. (Often you don't even know yourself.) Second, happiness is a by-product of feeling in control of your life, of making choices that suit your preferences. Expecting someone else to take care of meeting your needs does not lead to happiness.

Having someone to love and to love you back provides a fertile environment for happiness, but it doesn't guarantee it. You must still choose and act responsibly in a context of interdependence. Acting consistently on your own interest at the expense of your partner's needs and wishes is likely to cause resentment on their part, but consistently denying your own interests in an attempt to please them is just as likely to create resentment in you.

Be aware that you and your partner will have different interests and preferences from time to time.

This is inevitable. When differences occur, the most effective solutions will come from talking through all the possibilities and considering options that allow each of you to meet your most important needs.

Accept responsibility for your
actions and your own happiness.

DEPENDENCE/
INDEPENDENCE/INTERDEPENDENCE

Not only is it unnecessary for you and your partner to change in the same ways, it's not even desirable. One of the biggest threats to your vitality as a couple is the boredom that results from too much togetherness.

Be your own person and encourage your partner to do the same. You are unique and so is your partner. Preserve and develop that uniqueness. It need not detract from your relationship; in fact, it can make your relationship all the richer.

Respecting each other's need to continue growing as a separate person is a sign of maturity, and it will enhance what you both have to bring to the relationship.

> *Add richness to your relationship by*
> *sharing your individual interests.*

VALUES/NEEDS/EXPECTATIONS

No matter how well you know your partner, you are likely to discover some differences in values and expectations as your intimacy deepens and as you encounter new situations together for the first time.

For instance, new differences are likely to arise each time you face one of life's bigger transitions—having children, buying a house, changing jobs. By expecting differences to occur, you will decrease the likelihood of feeling dismayed or even betrayed.

Be prepared for some surprises.

VALUES/NEEDS/EXPECTATIONS

Don't get caught in the trap of comparing your needs and wants with your partner's to decide which are better. For instance, you may want a house in the country while they want a condo in the city. Both are valid desires and deserving of respect.

You don't have to agree with everything your partner needs and wants, but you do need to accept it as their choice. This willingness to accept legitimate differences is essential if you are to avoid power struggles and continual nit-picking.

> *Respect your partner's needs and*
> *wants that differ from yours.*

VALUES/NEEDS/EXPECTATIONS

It's fine to ask your partner for their support where you want it, but don't expect your partner to read your mind, to know what you need and want.

The conditioning of women to be nurturing may lead you as a woman to sacrifice your own needs, causing you to fail to assert yourself in a healthy, responsible way—and to resent your partner for meeting his own needs.

The conditioning of men makes it easier for you as a man to pursue your own needs and to assume your partner is doing likewise, causing you to be surprised (and irritated) when she expresses dissatisfaction with her life.

Both of you need to recognize the effects of male and female conditioning on this issue and work to overcome the strain it can cause in your relationship.

Take responsibility for meeting your own needs

VALUES/NEEDS/EXPECTATIONS

Some of your needs and wants are so important that you tend to think of them as having a constant priority. The truth is, all needs and wants are in a constant process of change. Some of the things that were of utmost importance to you as an adolescent have now faded and possibly dropped all the way off your list of priorities.

On a day-to-day level, you can see constant shifts in your needs and wants. For instance, if you haven't seen your partner for several days, the need to spend time with them may move to the top of your list—surpassing even basic needs like eating and sleeping. Coming together at such times can be extremely exciting and satisfying, but after being together for a while, other needs, such as eating, resting, or going to work, move back to the top of the list.

If you think your partner never changes, it just means you aren't keeping up with their internal changes—and you may one day be in for a very big surprise. You need to recognize that neither you nor your partner will maintain exactly the same preferences throughout the life of your relationship. This awareness can help you deal with whatever differences you've discovered about your needs and wants.

> *Recognize that your individual*
> *needs and wants will change*

VALUES/NEEDS/EXPECTATIONS

You probably chose your partner partly because you perceived that the two of you had some significant values in common. If you've been together very long, you've probably also noticed that even these common values aren't always in sync as your individual needs fluctuate in accordance with your unique experiences. Don't despair.

Communicate instead. It takes a lot of clear communication to keep each other abreast of your changing needs and wants. You'll experience both an immediate and a long-term payoff. Your relationship will stay vibrant as each of you brings new perspectives and new energy to the partnership.

Not communicating regularly about your kaleidoscope of needs is sure to bring some surprises and frustrations as you try to plan activities together based on outdated assumptions.

Deal constructively with your
differences and changes in needs

POWER/CONTROL

The use of power to get your way carries a heavy cost. It inevitably diminishes the less powerful person, breeds fear, and erodes trust. It also increases the chances that your partner will use their power inappropriately at some point in the future. No matter how subtle you try to be in your use of power, negative consequences will occur. You may try to remain unaffected on the surface, but if you feel oppressed by your partner's power or control, you're likely to keep score and look for the opportunity to strike back.

The use of power depends on how *both* of you deal with it. One can't exercise undue control without the cooperation of the other. And inevitably both of you lose when you give in to power games, because your relationship cannot thrive and prosper in that kind of environment.

> *Avoid using power to get what you want;*
> *fairness builds, power destroys.*

POWER/CONTROL

Using your love to control your partner will systematically diminish both the strength and the quality of the bond between you. If your partner fears losing your love if they fail to conform to your wishes, the very feelings of comfort and caring that form the basis of real love will be eroded.

You may think that manipulation is not as damaging as outright power plays, but your partner's feelings about you and about the relationship are likely to be affected in a negative way regardless of the manner in which you try to exercise control over them. No one likes feeling they're in a one-down position, no matter what the method of putting them there.

Never use your love to manipulate
or control your partner.

POWER/CONTROL

Make a habit of addressing problems in the relationship independent of your sexual relationship. While your sexual relationship can't be kept completely separate from the rest of your relationship, the sexual arena should not be a dumping ground for whatever frustrations, aggravations, or other issues exist between you and your partner.

It's also unreasonable to think that outside issues won't have any effect on sexual feelings, especially for you as a woman—where conditioning makes you vulnerable to being strongly affected. As a man, your conditioning allows you to separate sexual feelings from other feelings more easily, but it's critical for both of you to avoid making sex a part of the problem. If you can maintain a good sexual relationship, it can contribute toward effectively dealing with other issues.

Never use sex to punish your partner.

COMPETITION/COOPERATION

Building up your self-esteem at the expense of your partner's self-esteem will interfere with the easy flow of loving feelings and cause your partner to look for ways to get even. The kind of love that sustains a lasting relationship is one that causes both people to feel good about themselves.

Many couples treat every difference of opinion as a win-lose encounter. You may gain some momentary satisfaction from winning a point over your partner, but you can be sure you're creating a situation where both of you will eventually lose.

Avoid win-lose competition with your partner;
don't build yourself up at their expense.

COMPETITION/COOPERATION

You may feel competition with your partner is OK as long as you restrict it to certain areas while cooperating in others—but you may be kidding yourself. In fact, your basic underlying *attitude* toward your partner (a generally competitive attitude or a generally cooperative attitude) affects *all* your interactions.

Cooperating doesn't imply giving up your right to be your best and do your best at whatever is important to you; it simply means supporting your partner in being their best and doing their best as well. Remember that cooperating is aiming for win-win situations (where each of you feels good about yourself) instead of win-lose situations (where one feels good at the other's expense).

> *Go beyond just avoiding competition; actively cooperate with your partner.*

RESPECT/SELF-ESTEEM

You are a worthy person and you deserve to be loved unconditionally. Most of us confuse our worth with what we've achieved or what we've accumulated or the extent to which we live up to others' expectations. If your parents were wise enough and skilled enough to consistently affirm their love for you (even when they didn't like the way you were behaving), you can consider yourself extremely fortunate. Most of us were not so lucky. The net result is, few of us experienced enough unconditional love on a continual basis to develop a fundamental appreciation of our worth apart from the approval of others.

Regardless of your childhood experiences, you're a grown person now, and it's up to you to be a good parent to yourself. You will make mistakes and you will fail to meet expectations (your own and those of others), but this doesn't make you a failure or an unworthy person. It's perfectly OK to reject your behavior when you don't live up to your expectations, but it's not OK to generalize and reject yourself in the process.

If you don't love yourself unconditionally, it's unlikely you'll be able to love anyone else unconditionally. Rejecting yourself also makes it more difficult for others to love you unconditionally.

*Accept your basic worth and learn to
love yourself unconditionally.*

RESPECT/SELF-ESTEEM

Your body is an important part of your total person. Acknowledge the truly miraculous instrument that it is. It's also full of paradox. It's extremely durable *and* extremely fragile. It needs regular maintenance as surely as your car or any other personal possession. Don't ignore it until it gives you trouble.

Be gentle with your body. Learn to love it. Don't judge your body by unrealistic standards of appearance or functioning. You're not likely to treat it well when you don't like it. You can do more for your body when you feel compassionate toward it and when you appreciate what it does for you. It's the only one you've got, and with proper care, it will serve you well.

Take good care of your body.

RESPECT/SELF-ESTEEM

It's normal to have a more or less continuous conversation going on in your head about what has already happened, what's happening right now, and what you want to happen in the future. The way you talk to yourself, however, is very important. Your self-talk can be encouraging and life-supporting or it can be discouraging and even life-threatening.

In the process of growing up, most of us were criticized by parents and teachers who did their best to help us learn effective ways of behaving. They also praised us for positive behavior, but our most vivid memories are more likely to be of the critical voices. Unfortunately, many of us internalized these early authority figures, setting the tone for the way we talk to ourselves throughout our lives.

Since the way you talk to yourself was learned, it can be changed. It's appropriate to notice when your behavior falls short of what's desired and to make plans to do better next time, but it's not good to beat up on yourself. Habitually looking for something to criticize (or being overcritical about things that don't really matter) is highly self-destructive.

Perspective is crucial. You need to affirm your positive actions realistically, forgive yourself for shortcomings, give yourself encouragement, and allow yourself to dream of what might be.

Manage your self-talk.

RESPECT/SELF-ESTEEM

The image you hold of yourself is probably the single most important determinant of your behavior in all areas of life. Thinking well of yourself gives you the courage to take risks, to build strong relationships, and to persist in the pursuit of lofty goals when the chances of success look dim. Thinking poorly of yourself reduces the likelihood that you will even try to succeed at significant endeavors.

Self-esteem is not a fixed characteristic. It is learned, and it continues to change throughout your life. Everyone you interact with has the opportunity to add to your positive view of yourself or to diminish it.

Unfortunately, the world is full of people who are careless in the way they talk to others and who will diminish your self-esteem if you allow it. Don't give anyone the right to judge you and control your self-esteem.

Don't let others diminish your self-esteem.

RESPECT/SELF-ESTEEM

Notice how you react when your partner says something nice or pays you a compliment. Do you accept it graciously so that both of you can enjoy the moment? Or do you tend to discount it in some way?

If you somehow reject the gift of a positive stroke, the giver may feel rejected as well. Not only will you lose the benefit of this experience, but it may discourage your partner from giving positive strokes in the future.

Positive strokes are important far beyond the momentary satisfaction you get from them. They are energizing and life-giving. Work to overcome whatever embarrassing feelings they may produce in you and enjoy the good feelings they can bring.

Accept positive strokes without apology or denial.

RESPECT/SELF-ESTEEM

The conditioning you get in growing up as a male or a female sometimes makes it difficult for you to treat each other with mutual respect. A man may take a controlling attitude toward a woman and treat her more as a helpless, emotional child than as an equal. And a woman may take a mothering (smothering) attitude toward a man and treat him like an incompetent, thoughtless little boy.

Give your partner the respect and thoughtfulness every adult wants and deserves—regardless of who might happen to have more information in a given situation. There will be instances where you have more information about some particular subject or more experience with a particular activity than your partner, and you may be tempted to use this knowledge as a way to control them. You may gain a measure of control in the short run, but you will lose in the long run.

Respect for the strengths and abilities of your partner allows you to communicate in a way that is productive and brings you closer together.

Treat your partner like a full-fledged adult.

GENEROSITY/SUPPORT

Develop a spirit of generosity toward your partner. A significant part of loving is wanting what is best for your partner—which means wanting what *they* think is best for them, not what *you* think is best. When each of you can be generous in your support of each other's needs, you'll both be better satisfied with the relationship.

Learn to forgive yourself and your partner when either or both of you fail to live up to your expectations.

GENEROSITY/SUPPORT

Everyone needs at least one other person with whom they can share innermost thoughts without fear of being judged or rejected. Be that person for your partner.

This is especially important when you know they're struggling to express themselves around a difficult issue—and one or both of you are upset.

When your partner is upset, they may overstate or misstate their feelings. It's up to you to recognize this tendency and not get hooked into responding in such a way as to escalate those feelings.

When you're the one who's upset, you're likely to exaggerate a tendency we all have to some degree—that is, to overpersonalize what your partner says.

Each of you is likely to have times when you don't say exactly what you mean, so it's important to give each other the benefit of the doubt until both of you are less emotional.

Be a generous listener; interpret your partner's words in the best possible way.

GENEROSITY/SUPPORT

You don't need to keep a day-to-day score on how much you are giving versus how much you are receiving. But it's good to make an overall assessment of who gives most and who receives most in the relationship—taking into account words, deeds, and material things. If you find yourself on the receiving end most of the time, you may need to focus on the joys of giving to a greater extent.

It's important to be gracious in giving and in receiving. Both of you will benefit from freely demonstrating your love and caring.

Be a good giver as well as a good receiver.

GENEROSITY/SUPPORT

Be there for your partner. That's what a real friend is—always there when you need them, through good times and bad.

Don't think that loving your partner automatically makes you a good friend. Some people are lovers but not friends while others are friends but not lovers. The combination of being both friend and lover is the most powerful of all. Trust, caring, understanding—the common threads of friendship—are essential to mature love.

Be a good friend.

FAIRNESS/EQUALITY

You can't sustain deep trust (and the intimacy that comes from that trust) without having a sense of fairness and equality in the relationship.

If there's an imbalance of power and influence— regardless of whether you are in the one-up or one-down position—the bond of trust will be weakened. And without that bond, you're unlikely to be able to maintain the kind of intimacy you want.

On the other hand, when you are genuinely committed to fairness and equality and are willing to demonstrate that commitment in all areas of your lives together, your trust and intimacy will continue to grow.

> *Commit to a relationship based on fairness*
> *and equality with your partner*

FAIRNESS/EQUALITY

Don't be literal in your quest for equality. Trying to make sure each of you does exactly 50 percent of every household chore simply won't work. Likewise, having lengthy discussions about every expenditure of money won't ensure equality.

Let your partner know on a continuing basis that you're conscious of their needs as you make decisions and initiate actions. Establish your clear intention to treat your partner as an equal and your willingness to discuss the situation whenever they feel otherwise. The lack of a sense of equality in your relationship can cause resentments that lead to constant antagonism and haranguing.

Strive for a sense *of equality*

FAIRNESS/EQUALITY

A sense of fairness is important because it affects not only your feelings about your partner but also your feelings about yourself. It's a blow to your sense of self-worth if your contribution is not recognized and appreciated.

In order for your partner to hear and appreciate your feelings of unfairness, you need to express them in a straightforward, descriptive manner instead of a whining, complaining, or critical way. If your comments sound like an attack, they are likely to elicit a defensive, argumentative response from your partner or even a counterattack.

Your goal in discussing feelings of unfairness is to improve the situation, but a failure to communicate effectively can make things even worse. As with most difficult discussions, you will be more effective if you use "I" statements (describing your own feelings and actions) instead of "you" statements about your partner.

If it's your partner who is describing feelings of unfairness, you need to listen and acknowledge those feelings instead of rejecting their right to feel that way. This will increase the likelihood that the discussion will continue in a productive way instead of turning into a debate, with each of you trying to prove you're right.

> *Discuss any feelings of unfairness*
> *instead of letting them fester*

4

Back to the Day-to-Day Issues

We hope you feel better prepared to tackle the daily hassles of life now that you've gotten a sense of the deeper issues they so often represent. We're absolutely convinced that this probing of the deeper issues between you is the only way to resolve your disagreements. All the typical advice about how to "fight fair" really misses the point. Resolving some particular immediate dispute means nothing if you don't address and deal with the underlying, deeply felt values.

We're the first to admit that the day-to-day issues still take up a lot of time. That's because each of us comes to the relationship with our own agenda regarding the issues related to building a life together as a couple—and with our own opinions as to how these issues should be handled. Differences are inevitable, and it's essential that they be discussed and dealt with on an ongoing basis.

Don't kid yourself by thinking you know your partner's position on every issue. If you just assume you know what your partner thinks, you'll be wrong a lot of the time. And even when you're right, you probably won't understand *why* they feel the way they do. So it's essential to use those good communication skills you're working on and talk about your individual attitudes and beliefs. In this way, you can identify your differences and clarify what they mean—which is the first step to effectively managing them.

Of course, you're never going to settle your differences once and for all, because you and your relationship will continue to change over the years. Just when you think you've got things figured out, *wham*—you get surprised.

One of the most significant and dramatic areas of change for us has been the place of religion or spirituality in our lives. When I was a child, I dreamed of becoming a missionary. This goal had been set aside by the time we became a serious couple at age 17. Getting married and having a family became the new goal.

Although James had been active in church-related activities while growing up, he hadn't planned to make religion central to his life and livelihood. But his thinking changed during his first year of college, leading him to switch colleges and study to become a minister.

When we married, James was a preministerial college student, and we both expected his choice of occupation would dictate the future of our lives together. Then came another change —just as unexpected as the first. In his senior year, James decided to become a psychologist and shifted full-time into that field of study.

Ever since that time, the issue of spirituality has affected our daily lives in a multitude of ways, clearly demonstrating the ongoing nature of dealing with such core issues. Our joint focus on philosophy, psychology, and sociology has caused us to continually examine our values—discussing them, identifying them, and committing to them. This evaluation process was not always smooth; we did not always agree on every aspect of religion and spirituality. But as a result, much of our work for the past 20 years has been grounded in an ethical base that is significantly different from the organized religion of our earlier days.

There have been many other areas of change throughout our lives, most of them fairly typical of what happens in long-term relationships. For instance, our sex life (like that of most new relationships) pretty much took care of itself in the beginning. As the years went by and our demands and responsibilities grew, it required planning and commitment. When there was a lot of secrecy and distance between us, our sex life suffered. And when we developed real honesty, we discovered the excitement that comes from being completely open and vulnerable with each other. In the beginning, we were not very knowledgeable or creative in our expressions of sex, and I didn't take charge of my own satisfaction. But our attitudes and beliefs changed dramatically, creating significant changes in our sex life.

Another issue, closely associated with sex, is dealing with attractions to others. This issue is particularly challenging because it involves people outside the relationship. The changes in our attitudes and beliefs about this issue have been quite extreme. In the beginning of our relationship, James was so jealous that he didn't want me to dance with anyone else and was uncomfortable with any physical contact I might have with another man, even my own father. After marriage, James's attitudes changed and he relaxed his earlier concerns.

It's difficult to say exactly how and why this change took place—which is often the case. Many such changes are by-products of maturity. But it's essential that we be *open* to change. Some people fear change because it represents the unknown. Resisting change is shortsighted, since you can't effectively *prevent* change anyway. But *managing* change is possible and desirable.

The most significant change in our relationship stemmed from the issue of extramarital affairs. I had not been particularly jealous or suspicious in the beginning of our relationship, but I became extremely anxious when I began to suspect James's affairs. Openly facing this issue (about 20 years ago) brought about the most dramatic change of our lives.

We completely changed the way and the depth with which we communicated and the way we related to each other. We made a commitment to ongoing honesty about all issues affecting our marriage (including, of course, attractions to others). The trust that came from this kind of honesty has meant that since that time neither of us has felt anxious about the normal attractions that exist between men and women. We're able to acknowledge them, discuss them, and not feel the uncertainty that comes from wondering if your partner will deceive you by acting on an attraction.

These are only a few examples of the daily issues that every couple must face throughout their relationship. Others we'll cover in this chapter include dealing with friends, relatives, children, money, work, and play. While any one of these can be a major distraction to sustaining loving feelings on a day-to-day basis, they're even more important when viewed in light of the underlying issues they represent (as discussed in the previous chapter).

Since these issues make up the stuff you deal with every day, we've devoted a lot of space to addressing them. This is by far the longest chapter in the book. Some of these issues will be more critical to your own personal situation than others (and only you know which ones they are), so take what you need from the wide range of issues discussed. You'll find that relieving some of the strain from these daily stressors can allow you to free up the loving feelings that often get buried underneath.

SEX

If we were sufficiently attuned to our bodies and if we weren't inhibited by so many sexual shoulds and oughts, we would probably have sex more often in response to the normal sexual stimulation we receive from our internal and external environments.

Our modern life-style, with its focus on accumulating things and experiences, has dulled our ability to listen and respond to the subtle stream of messages from our bodies. Many of these messages are sexual in nature and could lead to sexual activities, but they are competing with many other stimuli for your attention. You must choose to amplify them to the point of acting on them and enjoying them in and of themselves.

Make a commitment to monitor and tend to your own sexual needs more carefully—first by simply paying attention and second by acting on what you notice. Be patient with yourself. This is simple, but it isn't easy.

Increase your sexual enjoyment
by simply paying attention.

{ **125** }

SEX

Physical foreplay can be an important part of a good sexual experience, but mental foreplay can be just as significant. Thinking ahead and planning ahead is probably the surest way to eliminate the *not-in-the-mood* response that often occurs when you surprise your partner with a sexual invitation.

Your thoughts condition everything you see and do. Don't wait for your partner or some external stimulus to prompt you to think about sex. Put it on your own agenda. And don't count on your partner always being able to shift mental gears whenever you get the urge. Tell them in advance you're thinking about it.

Try it right now. Plan a time and place for your next sexual encounter with your partner. Imagine in graphic detail how it will go. Call your partner and share your plan. The biggest risk is that you'll get them so excited, they won't be able to control themselves.

Use your brain to create the sex life you want

SEX

Work to make your lovemaking as good as possible, but don't expect perfection. It won't happen. Sometimes your best efforts to produce pleasurable feelings in your partner will not succeed. Sometimes carefully crafted plans to create a time and place for lovemaking simply don't work out. Give yourself credit for having good intentions—and know that tomorrow is another day.

You need to be both patient and persistent in improving your sex life. It didn't suddenly become the way it is, and it won't quickly change. Just beginning the process will be a step in the right direction.

*Accept that nothing—not even
your lovemaking—is perfect.*

SEX

Many men and women go through their entire lives without the ability to talk easily with each other about sex. Men have generally learned a locker-room language that objectifies women and isn't usually appropriate in a love relationship. Women, on the other hand, are more likely to have learned the technically correct vocabulary, but are sometimes less comfortable in talking about sex.

It's crucial that you be able to discuss any and all aspects of your sexual relationship. Start with whatever words you're accustomed to using and check your partner's acceptance of them. Keep trying new words and expressions until you find ways to refer to sexual acts and body parts with which both of you are comfortable.

> *Develop a sexual vocabulary*
> *that works for the two of you.*

SEX

The tremendous emphasis on the perfect figure or physique in our society has made it very difficult to feel good about your body. You may not feel sexy if you don't think you look sexy. But this is getting things exactly backward. In fact, you will look sexy when you feel sexy. So your focus needs to be on getting in touch with your sexual feelings.

A body that feels sensual is a beautiful body. You're as beautiful as you feel and act—especially when it comes to engaging in loving sex with your partner.

> *Appreciate your body and that of your partner as sexy—and attractive.*

SEX

Having an orgasm is usually the primary goal of having sex, but it needn't be the only one or even the most important one. Too much focus on performance, or on producing any specific sexual result, can keep you from responding naturally and spontaneously in the moment.

When you're thinking too much during sex, you're not completely present and aware of what's going on. Thinking about what should happen (or how often it should happen) is a distraction from being in touch with what *is* happening.

Remember that what matters is not how your sex life compares to some ideal but how satisfying it is to you and your partner.

Learn to go with the flow. Genuinely expressing your love, knowing that it will not always result in the same outcome, can be the best performance of all.

Don't be preoccupied with performance—
especially someone else's definition of it.

SEX

Good sex requires good teamwork. In any team situation, it's preferable to start with people who are individually talented, but that's no assurance that the team will perform well. You must also cooperate in order to reach your full potential.

The same is true of sex. You can get some measure of sexual satisfaction without the full cooperation of your partner, but if you want to achieve the best of what's possible, you had better learn to function as a team. This means having great clarity about what you're trying to do together and maintaining a high degree of sensitivity to each other as you proceed. It means sometimes leading and sometimes following—but always cooperating—because good sex is a team sport.

Always remember—
the best sex is based on teamwork.

SEX

Wash your genitals carefully every day, not because they're particularly dirty, but because they deserve good care.

Use the Boy Scout motto: Be prepared. The joy of sexual pleasure with your partner is certainly enhanced by feeling fresh and relaxed. And taking care of the basics in a conscious way can help create an open attitude toward sexual involvement.

Make good sexual hygiene a daily practice.

SEX

Oral sex can add a special dimension to your love-making. If your early conditioning led you to regard sex and genitalia as dirty, do yourself a favor: reconsider the issue from your adult perspective. Anything that you and your partner find mutually stimulating and satisfying can have a positive impact on your sex life.

Enjoy the added pleasures of oral sex.

SEX

Be a good animal. Follow your instincts.

The human anatomy is a thing of beauty. Appreciate the appearance of your unique bodies. Look without embarrassment or self-consciousness as long as you like.

Taste and smell are probably the most sensitive areas to talk about and in some cases the most important—at least if you enjoy oral sex. The odors you generate during sexual arousal are different. Whether you enjoy them will depend as much on your attitude as on the odors themselves.

Notice your partner's response to your touch. Ask about their reaction when you're not sure. Be explicit about how and where you like to be touched.

Revel in the sounds you make. Don't hold them in and don't be embarrassed by the unexpected ones. Sounds often provide important clues to what's going on. For instance, noticing the changes in your partner's breathing can be a good indicator of when they're nearing orgasm. Your ability to tune in to each other during sex can make the sexual experience better for both of you.

Use all your senses to enjoy and appreciate sex.

SEX

Openness to sharing your fantasies and desires is probably the best way to keep sex fresh and exciting. Too often we think that sex can only be really exciting when a relationship is new. There is certainly an element of truth in this belief if we're talking about sustaining the sheer level of excitement some of us experienced the first time we had sex. But nowhere is it written that sex must get increasingly dull and boring.

By communicating honestly about sex and other feelings as well, you can keep your sex life alive and well. It's the distance that's created when you hold back your thoughts and feelings that contributes to the loss of sexual excitement.

> *Be honest about what you like and don't like—what you want and don't want.*

SEX

While a leisurely sexual encounter with full expression of your loving feelings is great, it's not the only appropriate way to have sex. A quickie can be fun and satisfying if you're willing to view it that way. There's nothing wrong with a frantic session in the car if that's where the urge hits—and if you can do it safely.

It's nice when you and your partner want sex at the same time, but you can be sure there will be times when one of you simply isn't in the mood. A willingness to participate in your partner's desire for sex can have a very positive effect on your relationship. While your own sexual satisfaction is important, there's also pleasure to be derived from contributing to your partner's satisfaction.

Be flexible. Keep experimenting. Have fun.

Broaden your view of what's appropriate *sex*

SEX

Some things need to be controlled during sex. Locking the door makes sense if there are young children who might walk in unannounced. Turning off the radio makes sense if it distracts you. Playing romantic music is fine if it makes you more comfortable or masks some of your lovemaking sounds which others might hear.

At the same time, realize that the best sex can only happen when you let yourself go. Perhaps what you need to strive for is controlled abandon.

> *Don't try to exercise too much*
> *control during the sex act itself.*

SEX

Variety really is the spice of life. Regardless of how sexually aware or experienced you may be, there is always more to learn about this important part of a relationship. Sometimes we're unaware of sexual possibilities that can bring newness and variety to our lovemaking, and we settle for repeating whatever worked in the past. Even the best of routines gets boring if nothing new and different is ever introduced.

Don't fall into the trap of always having sex in the same position, at the same time of day, or in the same location. Don't make the sexual invitation in the same way all the time. You need not dampen your sexual enjoyment with a narrow range of sexual behavior.

There needs to be a basic agreement between the two of you to express any ideas or desires you may have. This doesn't mean you'll agree on every one of them, but just being open to considering anything your partner suggests allows for wonderful possibilities. By respecting each other's desires (as well as any reservations), you can continue to enrich your sex life through the years.

And if you want your partner to do something different sexually, you'll be more likely to succeed by saying what you'd like, not by focusing on what you don't like. Better still, change your own behavior in a way that might cause a change in your partner's behavior.

*Continue to explore new ways of
expressing your love sexually.*

SEX

What's the best kind of sex: spontaneous or planned? The answer is both.

Any ideas that sex should only be spontaneous and not planned are very misguided. After all, when you were starting your relationship, you planned time and situations to make sex possible. Planning for sex in no way diminishes the pleasure of the activity—and may, in fact, increase it because of the anticipation.

The afterglow of good sex is likely to remain for several days and there's a good chance that you and your partner will be inclined to spontaneously have sex while still under the influence of these feelings. However, other demands sometimes interfere with acting on that inclination until those feelings just slip away. If you let a lot of time go by (waiting for it to just happen), there's actually less likelihood that it will spontaneously happen. So at this point it's important to plan for sex.

Don't neglect sex in the course of
attending to other areas of life.

MAINTENANCE ISSUES

There is no fairy godmother; the responsibility for carrying out daily chores is up to the two of you. And it's essential that you fulfill such responsibilities as cleaning, cooking, and child care in a way that is based on fairness. You might think this is so obvious that it doesn't need special attention. It's true that most of us are basically fair-minded people who intend to carry our own weight in any situation. But funny things happen in a love relationship.

So it's good for you as a couple to talk about how these chores are being handled and what it means if there is an imbalance. Like many areas of the relationship, this is one that can affect the way you feel about yourself and your partner if left to take care of itself. Remember that when you have persistent problems about maintenance issues, the underlying (and more serious) issue is usually one of fairness and equality. Since you're likely to be more focused on your own contribution than on your partner's, it's possible for each of you to feel that you're doing more than your share.

To address your perceptions of fairness, make a list of all the maintenance issues you and your partner can think of. Be specific and try to cover everything: cleaning, shopping, yard maintenance, car maintenance, cooking, child care, earning money, budgeting money, social arrangements, and so on. Candidly discuss how each of you feels about the entire list. It's not necessary (or possible) to evenly divide all chores, but it's important to discuss your feelings about the way things are going and what changes may need to be made.

> *Do your fair share of the routine chores*
> *that all relationships require.*

MAINTENANCE ISSUES

The dirty work of daily life has to be done, and it's important that both of you feel satisfied with the way it's divided. You and your partner may have different opinions of the degree of unpleasantness attached to specific chores. You may think you deserve special credit for doing something you see as quite unpleasant while your partner may not appreciate your sacrifice because they don't see it as being so bad.

Part of the problem with undesirable chores is that the person doing them seldom gets any extra credit for doing something no one else wants to do. Usually, they're simply taken for granted and ignored. This attitude, of course, undermines whatever satisfaction might otherwise come from taking care of some of these basic tasks.

> *Remember—someone has to vacuum, dust,*
> *take out the garbage, and clean the toilets.*

MAINTENANCE ISSUES

One person may see taking care of maintenance tasks as an expression of love while the other may feel these routine chores are just that—routine chores—and may put little value on who does them.

It's not essential that you feel exactly the same way about how much these actions reflect your love, as long as each of you understands the degree of significance the other attaches to this behavior.

Without this kind of insight, you may miss your partner's effort to demonstrate their love through these actions.

Appreciate the ways in which these issues
may be seen as a demonstration of love.

MAINTENANCE ISSUES

You may tend to believe it's only what you do that counts—regardless of who is ultimately responsible for seeing that it's done. But it's important to recognize the contribution of the person who assesses a need, discusses it, and takes responsibility for making sure it gets done.

For instance, in the business world a manager may determine what is needed, make that need known, and follow up to see that it's done—while someone else actually does it. We easily acknowledge the contribution of the manager in that instance, but we often fail to see the same kind of contribution in our private lives.

If you're the one who feels responsible for seeing that most things get done, you're likely to feel the stress associated with this responsibility. This, of course, takes a toll on the relationship as you struggle under the constant pressure of staying on top of so many areas.

> *Fairly distribute the responsibility for seeing*
> *that maintenance issues are taken care of—*
> *regardless of who actually does them*

MAINTENANCE ISSUES

One indication of whether you and your partner are fairly distributing responsibilities is to watch the language you use to describe your actions. When you say you helped your partner do thus and so, it usually shows that your partner is the one who bears the responsibility for that particular area.

For instance, in our society men have been conditioned to assume primary responsibility for earning money and women have been conditioned to assume primary responsibility for the home. While this is changing, you may find that as a man you speak of helping out at home and as a woman you speak of helping to earn the income for the family.

You and your partner need to establish a clear understanding of which responsibilities are to be shared and which ones are primarily assumed by one of you, with the other simply helping. There's no absolute way these decisions should be made, only that they are mutually agreeable to the two of you and that you reevaluate them periodically to be sure no feelings of unfairness are building up.

Recognize that helping *with responsibilities is not* sharing *them.*

MONEY

You can't afford to leave money matters to chance. It's tempting to assume that you share similar attitudes about money as long as things are going along relatively smoothly. But that's precisely the time you need to talk.

Money is the source of a great deal of friction in most relationships because it reflects differences in attitudes and values and is related to power and control. You and your partner need to discuss your beliefs and attitudes about money *before* there's a financial crisis and commit to continuing discussions as your relationship progresses and circumstances change.

Ongoing, open discussion will help you deal with your inevitable differences about how to earn and spend money.

Thoroughly discuss your attitudes
about making and spending money.

MONEY

You or your partner may see earning money as being more significant than other maintenance tasks, and that perception may prevent a fair assessment of your respective contributions to the relationship.

The degree to which each of you brings income into the relationship may affect the balance of power between you if you fail to keep this particular contribution in perspective.

Many men and women still believe that earning money buys a certain relief from other basic responsibilities, but all responsibilities need to be considered when determining a fair distribution of effort.

Realize that issues around earning money
affect other areas of your relationship.

MONEY

Withholding information about money says more about your attitude toward your partner than about your attitude toward money. It may indicate that you don't trust your partner or that you don't value them as an equal.

This is one of the reasons money is such a volatile issue in most relationships. Whether you mean for it to or not, the way you relate to your partner about money matters sends a strong message about your respect—and even your love.

Never hide information from your
partner about money earned or spent.

MONEY

Don't allow one of you to become the boss in charge of money decisions. This doesn't mean that everything must be jointly decided—especially not routine money matters. But if one of you dictates the major decisions or controls the allotment of money, it's sure to create other problems in the relationship related to fairness and respect.

Money differences often reflect differences in the way you view financial security. For one of you, security may mean having more while for the other it may mean needing less. It may also reflect differences in values; one may be willing to give up significant amounts of time for other things in order to make money while the other places more value on having free time to use in other ways.

Negotiate your differences about money.

WORK

Work is likely to be a dominant factor in your relationship as a couple since it's a necessary means of earning a livelihood—in addition to being a source of stimulation and pride.

Differences about the role of work in your lives can create tension and disagreements about your use of time and energy—as well as your use of money. Don't let work become a bone of contention between you, with one (or both) of you resenting the other's job and each of you vehemently defending the rightness of your position.

Instead of getting caught up in an endless debate over work itself, identify and address the underlying issues—which probably include feelings about self-esteem, fairness, control, and differing needs and expectations.

Discuss your attitudes and feelings about the place of work in your lives.

WORK

While you may be like most people in that you say your family is more important than your work, the real test is whether this is reflected in the ways you spend your time and energy. You may see work as a necessary evil while your partner sees it as the clearest path to self-fulfillment. You may see it only as a task while your partner sees it as the primary determinant of who they are as a person.

Maintaining a good balance between home and work is a critical challenge in sustaining a long-term relationship. You need to acknowledge that work can have both a positive and a negative impact on home life—and that home life can have both a positive and a negative impact on work. The key is to reinforce the positive effects each area can have on the other, while decreasing the negative ones.

Constantly assess the impact of work on your personal lives and on your relationship

TIME

No time is as important as now. It's simplistic, but true, that now is all you've got; the past is gone, and when the future gets here, it will be now. So you need to pay attention to your relationship each day; don't depend on memories of the past or dreams for the future to see you through.

Living in the moment does not mean living only for whatever you can get out of the moment without regard to consequences. That's living for the moment. There's a big difference between the two. Living *for* the moment is living irresponsibly, without thought or awareness—a kind of mindlessness. Living *in* the moment is living with full awareness and appreciation of life.

Live in the moment, not in the past or in the future.

TIME

Don't allow your love relationship to function on automatic; give it the kind of attention you give to any important area of your life. You may be caught up in the romantic idea that time for your relationship should just happen. Maybe you don't like the idea of planning for love or scheduling time together. But try to overcome your resistance. You schedule other really important things in your life; why not time for each other?

You may feel it's OK to have very little time together as long as whatever you do have is quality time. But quantity is important too—specifically, having consistent intervals of time together in order to stay in touch and avoid becoming strangers.

If you're so pressured that you *never* have time together without scheduling it, this may say something about your natural inclination to be together, as well as the degree of importance you place on the relationship.

Mostly, people spend their time on the things in their lives that they deem to be important. So if your relationship is important, you'll see to it that you make time for it—even if it requires scheduling.

Don't hesitate to schedule time for each
other if it isn't happening naturally.

TIME

Be honest with your partner about your own needs for time alone. Invite them to express their needs in return. Together you can work out the best way to meet both of your needs.

Your need for alone time will change as you and your life circumstances change. Your needs will not necessarily change in the same direction or at the same pace as those of your partner. Some trade-offs are probably essential.

You've no doubt had some periods in your life when you were involved with others but would have preferred to be alone. You've probably also noticed that our society expects committed couples to spend a lot of time together and that many people are suspicious of the commitment if partners spend a lot of time apart. It will not work to let others dictate this crucial part of your relationship. It will also not work to establish a pattern and expect it to last forever.

Obviously, it's equally important that you respect your partner's need for time alone. Each of you will need to appreciate that this doesn't diminish love. In fact, the increased opportunities for reflecting on your life (and your love) when you're alone are likely to strengthen your appreciation for your partner and for the relationship you share.

Respect your individual needs for time alone

ATTRACTIONS TO OTHERS

You probably realize it's natural for your partner (and yourself) to find others attractive. Nevertheless, it's probably something you don't want to think about. You'd like to believe it won't happen, so you may convince yourself that somehow your relationship will be different.

If you try to deny the possibility of attractions, you send a subtle (or not so subtle) signal to your partner that you don't want to know about any of their feelings of attraction toward others. Since attractions are both normal and inevitable, you're in essence sending a message that says, "Lie to me; pretend you're never attracted to anyone else." This, of course, causes other problems related to honesty that can have serious consequences for your relationship.

Accepting the reality of attractions to others is the first step toward being able to keep them in perspective. If you see attractions as a direct threat to your love (thinking that if your partner loved you they would never be attracted to anyone else), you're granting power to attractions that they would not otherwise possess.

Accept that attractions to others are normal and inevitable, no matter how much you love each other.

ATTRACTIONS TO OTHERS

Attractions are not, in and of themselves, a problem. The problem comes when they are acted on. And the best way to decrease the likelihood of that happening is to honestly discuss this issue and your feelings about it on an ongoing basis.

Attractions become a much greater threat to the relationship whenever acknowledging them is taboo. If you can't talk about these feelings, they become your own private secret and are likely to grow in intensity and desire. But openly discussing your feelings brings a degree of reality to the issue that leads to a more sensible and responsible way of thinking, which in turn reduces the desire to act on the attractions.

Talk honestly about your attractions and how to deal with them in order to reduce their power and effect.

ATTRACTIONS TO OTHERS

You may have every intention of being monogamous and not becoming involved in an extramarital affair. (In fact, most people profess their intention to be monogamous when they marry and express disapproval of affairs.) This does not, however, prevent you from being vulnerable to having an affair.

Realistically, no one is immune—including you and your partner—from getting involved in an affair at some point during marriage. So it's essential that you recognize this risk and deliberately focus on the consequences involved in an affair. The tendency to focus only on the excitement and positive feelings often blocks your ability to think clearly or to contemplate the repercussions of acting on those feelings.

While you may rationalize that an affair brings some temporary pleasure without long-term consequences, you're kidding yourself. The dishonesty and deception inherent in having an affair *will* affect your relationship and are likely to cause serious problems—whether or not the affair is ever discovered.

Be aware of the dangers in acting on your attractions.

ATTRACTIONS TO OTHERS

Your ideas about extramarital affairs (who has them, why, and who is to blame) are likely to be based on a very personal view of this issue. You may believe that affairs happen only because of a particular lack in the individual or a particular lack in the marriage. But affairs happen to all kinds of people in all kinds of relationships—and you can't fully understand why they happen by looking only at your own marriage.

This is such an emotionally charged issue that you may not want to think about it unless you absolutely must. But if either you or your partner has an affair, you will need to try to think as clearly as possible, despite the emotions. In order to recover, you will need a great deal of information, understanding, and perspective. Overcoming the emotional impact involves getting beyond personal blame and understanding what happened in the context of society as a whole.

Contrary to popular belief, ours is not a monogamous society. While society appears to uphold monogamy, there are many societal factors that actually serve to support and encourage affairs. (A more thorough guide to understanding and recovering from affairs is provided in our earlier book, *The Monogamy Myth.*)

> *Recognize that recovery is possible*
> *if an affair does take place.*

FRIENDS

You can't reasonably sit back and hope your partner doesn't have and won't make any friends of the opposite sex. And you also can't reasonably dictate that this never happen. What you can do is to openly discuss your individual feelings about opposite-sex friendships.

If you try to isolate your partner's friends or push them to the fringes of your life, you'll exaggerate their importance, creating even more problems. Instead, you can integrate these people into your social life as a couple. This doesn't mean that all your friends have to be joint friends, but it does mean that they aren't kept as a completely separate part of your life—which only increases the likelihood that they will adversely affect your primary relationship.

> *Confront the issue of opposite-sex*
> *platonic friendships head-on.*

FRIENDS

Allow your friends to complement your primary relationship, not compete with it. Whenever your relationship with your friends is seen as a threat to your love relationship, everybody loses. If you don't want to walk a tightrope between the two, you'll need to take a mature attitude toward a workable balance.

Women tend to complain that men *do* too much with their friends while men tend to complain that women *talk* too much with their friends. In each instance, the underlying issues are commitment versus freedom or dependence versus independence—as well as issues of fairness and respect.

So instead of getting bogged down in focusing on friends (as if they're the only source of the problem), you will make much more headway in resolving this issue if you're honest with yourself and your partner about the core issues mentioned above. And be sure to talk about these issues in terms of "I feel" or "I wish" rather than being judgmental and blaming ("you shouldn't" or "you always").

> *Don't let your same-sex friends cause you*
> *and your partner to feel like enemies*

FRIENDS

Don't fall into the trap of thinking that once you've become a couple, all new friends must be "couple friends." It's great to find other couples that both of you like, but it's too restrictive to think that all new friends must come in the form of couples. Finding couples where both of you genuinely like both of them requires time and patience. So don't try to force every new friendship into this mold.

Both of you can enjoy a friend who is not part of a twosome. If you're honest with yourself, you know that you present a slightly different side of yourself to people when you're alone than when you're with your partner. The same is true of others, so those friendships you form as a couple with single people have a special richness.

Be flexible in your approach to developing new friends as a couple.

RELATIVES

Put your partner first when dealing with both friends and relatives. This advice doesn't mean cutting off your close relationships with others. It simply means being clear about your primary commitment.

Developing a good, long-term relationship requires all the commitment and determination that you can possibly muster. Too many instances of abandoning your partner when the chips are down will inevitably erode the chances for sustaining a lasting love.

Make your partner your first priority.

RELATIVES

Let your family know of your commitment to your partner. Be subtle when possible, but direct when necessary. They need to understand the priority you give to your relationship. They will be more likely to be supportive and less likely to express negative feelings if they're clear about your commitment.

It's also important that you guard against letting other family members dictate your relationship. While they may not deliberately sabotage it, they can cause substantial problems if they presume to advise you on what's best for the two of you.

Another potential problem to guard against is that of relatives heaping unwarranted criticism on your partner. While their criticism may not be malicious, you need to squelch these attacks as soon as they appear. Your most effective approach is not to defend or debate but to ask that they show you respect by giving you credit for your choice of partner. You need to make it clear that you interpret their attacks on your partner as an attack on your judgment, and that you expect your judgment to be respected.

Establish clear understanding with other family members.

RELATIVES

In the best of relationships, your bond gives you the strength and independence to be expansive and intimately involved with other family members. If you are not clear about your commitment to each other, you may be threatened by even casual relationships with other family members.

When there's a conflict between the needs of your partner and those of your family, you'll need to be as thoughtful as possible in seeking a resolution that is as fair as possible to both parties. It can cause a significant strain on your relationship if you feel you constantly have to choose between your partner and others in your family.

*Be understanding of your individual needs
to maintain family connections.*

RELATIVES

Making major decisions about how you live as a couple includes determining how close you will live to your respective relatives. Maybe your parents want you to live nearby and put a great deal of pressure on you to do that. Maybe you feel fearful of moving away from your parents, as if you're abandoning them.

These may be very deep issues for you to resolve since they go to the very heart of your individual value systems. But it's one of many decisions that must be made on the basis of clear, mature thinking about your life as a couple and the impact of other forces on the course of your love.

Deliberately address the issue of the degree to which family members will be an integral part of your lives.

RELATIVES

There are sure to be differences in the importance each of you places on staying in touch with your families of origin. It's tempting for the one who wants closer family connections to be critical of the one who is less inclined to pursue family involvements. And it's equally tempting for the more private partner to resent the other's pressure to conform to their wishes.

Don't insist that your partner think and behave exactly as you do. Every family activity does not have to be undertaken together. Each of you can maintain whatever degree of contact with family members fits your needs—as long as it does not significantly take away from your contact with each other.

You face a special challenge, of course, in dealing with holidays. Don't assume that you have the same family traditions about celebrating holidays; discuss your families' styles with each other and explore the possibilities for coping with the inevitable differences.

Remember that there is no right or wrong way to celebrate holidays—only differences in preferences and expectations. Respect your past ways of doing things, but decide together how you want to design your own celebrations as a couple, establishing your own family traditions.

*Include your partner in family
traditions, but don't force it.*

CHILDREN

This may be the most challenging task you face as a couple—honestly dealing with whether and when to have children. While ideas about having children may change, it's preferable to share your feelings before getting married so you start with a clear understanding of where each of you stands. If you agree on whether you want to have children, that's a good start. If not, the situation calls for a great deal of clear thinking and rational discussion—because this is one of the few issues you face as a couple for which there is no good compromise.

Even if you agree on having children, deciding *when* to have them can create another major dilemma. You will no doubt consider work and money issues, along with other life-style issues. And you're likely to see age as a factor with regard to the biological clock.

But it's also important that you maintain some openness to the realistic unpredictability of having children. Despite the preferences or decisions the two of you make, you may have an unintended child or be unable to conceive a child. So it's essential that you make every effort to communicate clearly and effectively about all aspects of having children.

Thoroughly discuss your feelings about children

CHILDREN

Don't underestimate the extent of the changes that result from having children. This is a life-altering experience that has a significant impact not only on your relationship but on all other areas of your life: use of time, use of money, social life, work life, friends, extended family, and the other activities that give meaning to your life.

Be realistic. Having a child may bring you closer together; it can also drive you apart since very few new parents are truly prepared for the inevitable stresses a child brings to the relationship. Even the most wanted and planned-for addition to the family creates enormous tension between the two of you.

Recognize that children
dramatically affect your relationship

CHILDREN

Developing a new love relationship is complicated enough in its own right. Starting out with children presents additional stress and difficulty for both the biological parent and the stepparent. The full scope of this challenge isn't always evident at first. It's easy for everyone involved to be on their best behavior for a while, but soon differences in values and personal habits begin to erode the good humor of those family members who didn't choose the new relationship in the first place.

Creating a blended family is a still greater challenge and probably calls for an exceptional degree of maturity and commitment on the part of both partners. Young children in particular are often still trying to adjust to the loss of their first family at the time when they're being asked to accept a new authority figure in their lives. Some resistance is normal and understandable.

You can prevent or at least minimize some of these problems by honestly discussing them in advance. You'll also cope more effectively with those that do arise if you and your partner are clearly committed to dealing directly with them.

Deal honestly with your feelings
if one of you already has kids.

CHILDREN

You and your partner are sure to approach child-rearing with differing mind-sets based on how you were raised. So don't expect that you will magically agree on how to raise your kids. Even the experts don't agree on all aspects of child-rearing, so you and your partner are sure to have differences and conflicts.

It's tempting to think that your differences will just work themselves out as you go along. But you need to acknowledge them and address them on a current basis in order to keep them from getting out of hand.

While you no doubt wish there were a way to avoid all disagreements about how to raise kids, that's not realistic. If you accept that this is a tough job that requires the best input from both of you, you can use your differences to reach creative solutions that are better than either of you could discover alone.

*Expect that you will have different
ideas about how to raise kids.*

CHILDREN

If you fail to anticipate and sensibly discuss your differences about raising kids, each of you is likely to become rigid about your beliefs, causing you to be so polarized that being right becomes more important than being effective parents.

You also need to guard against competing with each other for the child's affection. If you become jealous of your partner's relationship with a child or jealous of their parenting ability, you are using the child to drive a wedge between the two of you.

Your feelings about each other as parents affect your feelings about each other in general. You can't be in a battle with your partner about child-rearing and be harmonious in other areas of your life.

Besides the cost to your relationship, the children pay a price as well. Children are very quick to pick up on the friction and competition between parents about how to handle parenting—and they're sure to be affected

While children can't sort through all the dynamics involved, this kind of home environment causes them to feel uncertain and anxious. The impact on your children of an ongoing battle between the two of you will be worse than the impact of following either of your conflicting positions about how to handle child-rearing.

> *Don't let child-rearing issues become*
> *a battleground between you*

CHILDREN

While being parents can be a very special and important part of your identity, it's critical that you also maintain a sense of yourselves as a loving couple.

You need to avoid falling into the habit of thinking of your partner primarily in terms of their role as a parent. Some couples begin calling each other Mom and Dad and continue it for many years—even when the children are not around or long after they're out on their own. Referring to your partner in this way diminishes your sense of them as your sexual partner and your companion in life.

Maintain a sense of being a loving
couple, not just parents.

CHILDREN

When you're in the midst of raising kids, it may be hard to foresee the day when they will be grown and you'll be alone as a couple to continue your lives together. Too much reliance on the kids as the basis for your relationship may leave you with little in common after the kids are gone.

This empty-nest period can provide new opportunities for enjoying life together—or it can stimulate feelings of despair and loneliness as you realize that your role as parents was the only bond that held you together. This doesn't necessarily mean you'll get a divorce, but it's likely to mean that your relationship will be pretty empty and meaningless—more practical than pleasurable.

> *Think ahead toward the time when your*
> *children will be grown and gone*

PLAY/RECREATION

Play serves important functions beyond the sheer enjoyment of the moment. It provides a way to engage others and therefore a means to develop relationships. It's also a rich source of learning and development—a means by which we define ourselves in relation to the world.

Unfortunately, spontaneous play in which the imagination plays a major role is typically seen as the province of young children. As we grow older, we're taught to play structured games with clear rules and usually with clear winners and losers. The sad truth is that much adult play is not really play at all. It's fierce competition that often results in more aggravation than enjoyment.

Rest assured, however, you never lose your capacity to play. You may have buried it deep inside, but it's there, waiting for you to let it out. Watch for the impulse to play and act on the next one that comes along. Encourage your partner to do the same.

Seize every chance to recapture the playfulness you had as a child.

PLAY/RECREATION

While you need a lot of adult communicating and relating to sustain a mature love relationship, you also need to take care of the child in each of you.

The kind of happiness that comes from having fun together is just as important as the quiet sense of happiness that results from deeper sharing. Your ability to participate in open, spontaneous joy can get smothered by your joint responsibilities unless you deliberately protect it.

You also need to acknowledge your childlike feelings of sadness and disappointment. These feelings are a natural part of dealing with the inevitable losses in life; hiding them will only create distance.

Nurture the child in yourself and your partner.

PLAY/RECREATION

Don't take yourself too seriously. Yes, there are many serious aspects to life, but overemphasizing life's difficulties brings an unnecessary heaviness to your overall attitude. You need to learn to laugh at yourself and at some of the things that happen to you in the course of routine living. There's great physical and emotional benefit in a full-blown belly laugh.

Your feelings about yourself and about your partner depend to a great extent on your basic attitude toward life—whether you see the glass as half full or half empty. Like everyone else, you will have good times and bad times. If you can maintain a sense of humor through the bad times, you will be able to keep a more positive perspective on life

Don't forget to laugh

PLAY/RECREATION

Sex is important, and you should take it seriously, but not too seriously. Hopefully, whatever apprehensions and misunderstandings you may have about sex in the early stages of involvement will give way to a relaxed enjoyment of sex in a loving relationship. This transition is more likely to occur when you're open to a wide variety of sexual interactions, including the pleasure of just messing with each other. (If you don't know what this means, go to a zoo and watch the gorillas' grooming activity: gently picking at, nudging, and generally touching each other.)

There's a childlike sense of openness and play to this kind of activity. While it's not strictly sexual, it involves a degree of sensuality that may or may not result in sexual activity. This kind of fooling around might feel silly or demeaning if there's tension or friction in the relationship. But in a relationship with free-flowing feelings of love, it can add an extra dimension of pleasure and closeness.

> *Let your lovemaking contribute to the fun in your lives; don't let sex become too serious.*

PLAY/RECREATION

Being a responsible adult is serious business. Making a decision to spend your life with another person is one of the most demanding commitments you'll ever make. It is compounded by the decision to have and raise children together. To be successful at both requires a high level of responsibility, but it does not require that you give up play.

In fact, becoming preoccupied with your responsibilities can diminish your ability to meet them. They can become so heavy in your mind that you seldom feel like playing even when an opportunity presents itself. Lighten up. Don't make life more serious than it is.

Guard against the deadening effects
of being responsible to the point
that you push play off your agenda.

PLAY/RECREATION

A great way to reclaim your natural bent toward playfulness is to observe and play with young children. Believe it or not, you were once just as playful as they are, and you can regain some of that playfulness if you let go of some of your learned inhibitions.

You need to appreciate that being an adult and being responsible don't have to be at the expense of being playful. In order to be a well-rounded person, you need to balance all aspects of your life, including play.

Imitate young children; they're masters at play.

PLAY/RECREATION

The pace of modern life doesn't always leave time for play. Yet everyone needs an activity they can engage in on a regular basis simply for the fun, relaxation, and enjoyment they get out of it. You'll be more effective at work and in your relationships if you find an activity that renews and refreshes you. If it's a physical form of play with aerobic benefit, that's a bonus. You'll be a better lover if you're physically toned and fit.

Don't be discouraged if you don't have any form of play that you enjoy at the moment, and don't assume that there is no play for you. Keep looking until you find an activity that draws you back again and again because you enjoy it, not just because it's good for you.

Find your play and help your partner find theirs.

PLAY/RECREATION

If you and your partner enjoy the same form of play, by all means go for it, but don't insist on always playing together. Often, two people who love each other very much don't enjoy the same forms of play; or even when they like the same activity, they don't enjoy doing it together. If that's the case with you, you may envy couples who seem to love playing together. Don't be so sure they have it better.

Remember the words of Mae West: "Too much of a good thing can be wonderful." And remember—she was wrong. Life is about balance. Too much of anything (even togetherness) becomes toxic at some point.

So recognize that it's also OK to have fun separately; you can share with your partner the enjoyment you derive from independent play, and you can take a genuine interest in whatever they're doing as well. You may derive more benefit from this kind of sharing than from playing together.

This means you must take a grown-up view of play. Pursue independent play as long as it doesn't place an inordinate burden on your relationship. It may actually renew your enthusiasm for the play that you share with your partner.

Include your partner in your favorite form of play when possible, but don't force it.

PLAY/RECREATION

If you feel bored, consider that you may be boring yourself (as well as your partner). Devote some significant time to discovering new sources of enjoyment. It will pay rich dividends in your relationship and in your overall life.

Be careful not to limit your vision of what is possible or appropriate in terms of play or recreation. If you're thinking only in terms of things you did when you were young, you may be missing a wide range of options. Go beyond thinking only about what you might enjoy; try to get in touch with whatever intuitive gut feelings you might have that draw you toward some particular interest. Above all, stay open to new possibilities.

Be creative in finding new interests and sources of joy.

RELIGION/SPIRITUALITY

Your emotional and spiritual experience of life is an integral part of who you are as a person. You've developed a belief system that determines what meaning you assign to the things you experience firsthand and the things you see other people experiencing. You may have found that your partner's belief system is different from yours, making it difficult for the two of you to derive spiritual benefit from the same practice.

It's not necessary that you and your partner pursue the same spiritual life. Don't give up the beliefs that have meaning to you and don't ask your partner to embrace yours at the expense of their own. Either course will likely lead to resentment. Remain open to modifying and expanding your belief system as you learn more about life. Since no one has a corner on the meaning of life, you can only gain by respecting your partner's way and learning from it.

The one thing you can surely celebrate together is the spiritual dimension of a powerful and pervasive love.

Nourish your emotional and spiritual life.

RELIGION/SPIRITUALITY

You are part of the web of life—a tiny part, but an important part nonetheless. You can sustain an appreciation of the magnificence of life by simply spending time in natural settings, by observing other living things making their way in the world.

Rekindle your sense of wonder and your curiosity through regular encounters with nature. It will give you a respite from your daily routine and a useful perspective from which to view your own problems.

Stay close to nature.

LIFE-STYLE PREFERENCES

If you fail to discuss your general attitudes about life-style, you're likely to assume your partner shares your preferences—which is a very dangerous way of proceeding. As your relationship progresses, you're sure to discover many differences, and you may find it difficult to reconcile the disparity between your individual hopes and dreams.

Don't wait until you have a clear vision of your life together. Go ahead and explore your individual ideas as a way of developing a view of life that accommodates the most important criteria for each of you. This doesn't mean you have to agree on everything, only that you know and understand both your own and your partner's primary desires about how to live your lives together.

Be honest with yourself (and with your partner) about your image of the kind of life-style you prefer

LIFE-STYLE PREFERENCES

You may find it very difficult to accept, or even to understand, how your partner could have some of their attitudes about life-style. Guard against the tendency to assume that their preferences are wrong just because they're different from yours. If you insist on proving that your way is best, you'll only compound the problem.

Differences in life-style preferences reflect one of the most fundamental core issues—the set of beliefs that each of you holds about what gives meaning to life. Your deeply held values have been formed at an unconscious level throughout your life and are not easily changed, especially by argument or debate. Reassessing your values is a gradual process that only succeeds through rational analysis and nonjudgmental discussion.

You will need to use your best communication skills to talk through this issue. And you will need to respect each other's values as legitimate while focusing on ways to accommodate your differences.

Acknowledge that there is no right or wrong way to live.

LIFE-STYLE PREFERENCES

Just when you think things are rolling along just fine, your partner may surprise you (or you may surprise them) by making a major switch in attitude about how to live. Career burnout and midlife crisis are among the more common of these changes. But even when the changes are not so drastic, either of you is likely to experience shifts in attitudes that cause you to rethink the course of your life.

For instance, you may be motivated for many years by a particular goal, such as having a house of a certain size in a particular neighborhood, only to find that it's not what you thought it would be once you've attained it. Similarly, working to achieve a certain level of income often brings with it shifts in habits, attitudes, and desires which are seldom envisioned as part of the original goal.

You can prevent a major upheaval by constantly staying attuned to your individual preferences as they change. Once again, communication is the key;

you can't assume things will always stay the same, and you can't read your partner's mind, so you'd better talk about your changing ideas before they create turmoil and uncertainty.

> *Be prepared for your preferences*
> *to change throughout your lives.*

5

A Positive Approach to
Your Negative Reactions

*D*on't be discouraged if you still occasionally have some negative reactions to the differences between you and your partner. Naturally, we'd all like to avoid feeling angry or hurt or resentful. But there will be times, despite your best efforts to deal with both the core issues and the day-to-day issues, when each of you has strong reactions to your differences. Some reactions may be easy to observe, such as anger or criticism; others may go underground in the form of hurt or resentment. Either way, they cause a great deal of stress to each of you individually as well as to your relationship.

So accept that you'll sometimes have these feelings—but don't just sit and stew; get about the

business of dealing with your feelings as constructively as possible. At this point you may not be able
to imagine how you can constructively deal with
your negative reactions, but that's what this chapter is about. You'll learn how to apply reason to
your emotions. You'll see that some emotions don't
stand up too well when confronted rationally.
You'll also see how self-defeating it can be to let
your negative reactions control you. One of the key
issues discussed in this chapter relates to the question "Would you rather be right or be in a loving
relationship?" It's critical that you not lose sight of
this perspective; it can help you control your negative reactions.

We've gone through many stages of reacting to
differences in our own relationship. In the early
days, I was more likely to feel anger, but I didn't
express it toward James. Slamming doors and "rat-
tling those pots and pans" were favored outlets.
James's early reactions were to hide his frustration
from me and moralize with other men about what
a pity it was that "all women are so emotional."

Later on, James was more likely to react with
criticism while I was more likely to silently harbor
feelings of hurt and resentment. Still later, I be-

came more likely to react with criticism while James's reactions were more likely to be based on hurt.

We're finally coming to a point of diminishing the impact of any of these reactions by talking about them instead of acting them out. This seems to work best in getting past them and on to whatever issues created the feelings in the first place.

If left to fester, negative reactions can take on a life of their own. In fact, reactions of anger or hurt can cloud the picture so much that you lose sight of whatever problem gave rise to the reactions in the first place. You can become so intent on justifying your reactions that nothing else matters. Meanwhile, your relationship is being damaged more and more every day that you dwell on your negative feelings.

One place to look for insight into the way you deal with differences is to reflect on what you learned from observing your parents while growing up. Even those of us who promised ourselves we would never fight like our parents often do exactly that when we're faced with similar circumstances.

You're not helpless to change your patterns of reacting to differences. It starts with a willingness to stop and look at what you're doing and the impact it's having on your relationship. If it's making things worse instead of better, common sense tells you to try something different. This reflects a saying from transactional analysis: "The way you are may be your parents' fault; but if you stay that way, it's your own fault."

The ideas in this chapter will help you get a clearer sense of how you can handle your negative reactions in ways that will avoid some of their damaging effects on your relationship. One thing we believe deeply: the cost of ignoring differences is far greater than that of dealing with them honestly and constructively.

CONFLICT

It's highly unlikely that you and your partner will have identical attitudes, beliefs, and preferences about how to conduct your lives, so some conflict is inevitable. This is neither good nor bad in and of itself. What matters is the way you deal with your differences. Trying to ignore them may get you beyond the immediate situation but will increase the likelihood of bigger trouble in the future.

*Accept that conflict is a natural
part of healthy relationships*

CONFLICT

Generally speaking, it's best to talk about differences as they occur. This gives you and your partner the best chance of accurately expressing your thoughts and feelings about a particular issue. Exceptions to this rule are:

- 🍋 when your feelings are so strong that you don't trust yourself to express them responsibly.
- 🍋 when you know your partner is not in a frame of mind to hear you.
- 🍋 when there are other people present and you or your partner would be embarrassed to talk openly in front of them.

Deal openly with differences in a timely way.

CONFLICT

Never use your intimate knowledge of your partner's vulnerabilities to gain advantage in an argument or to put them down in any way. Deal with whatever problem is on the table; don't try to get the upper hand temporarily by preying on your partner's weaknesses. It will always do harm to the relationship

Stick to the issue at hand

CONFLICT

If you insist on being right at the expense of your partner, you're paying a heavy price—one you probably wouldn't choose to pay if you considered the consequences. Always being made to be the loser or to be wrong in a disagreement will slowly kill your partner's love.

Make it a priority to thoroughly understand your partner's point of view. Many conflict situations escalate in intensity because neither partner can stop trying to win their own position long enough to understand the other.

If you win while your partner loses, then in essence you both lose. A sense of fairness is essential for loving feelings to survive.

*Decide whether you'd rather be right
or be in a loving relationship*

ANGER

Feeling angry in response to a particular incident or situation is reasonable and understandable. But carrying around a load of angry feelings just beneath the surface, ready to erupt at any time, is a sign of a far more serious problem (almost certainly a sign that the real problem is one of the core issues described in chapter 3).

Once you determine that the source of your anger is a given situation, deal with that situation as quickly as possible so it doesn't become a deeper problem. It's also critical that you express your anger in a way that resolves the feelings and allows you to let them go.

While individual ways of expressing anger vary, as a man you're more likely to show your anger by yelling, and as a woman you're more likely to show yours by crying. Neither sex responds well to these typical expressions of anger. The most effective way to deal with your anger is to describe your feelings rather than acting them out.

Accept that occasional feelings of anger are normal, but guard against feelings of constantly simmering anger.

ANGER

You probably feel that you never choose to be angry—your partner *makes* you angry. In reality, nobody can force you to feel any particular emotion at a given time. Your interpretation of whatever they have said or done (not just the event itself) plays a big part in determining whether or not angry feelings will result.

You may have a very difficult time thinking clearly when you feel angry, but this is precisely what's needed. You need to understand the causes of your anger instead of just giving in to the feelings. If you react without thinking, you're likely to regret it later.

Take responsibility for your own feelings of anger.

ANGER

When you're angry at your partner, you may have an impulse to strike out at them. This is a normal human reaction, but you don't have to act on it.

Never hit (or in any way physically harm) your partner; there's no place for physical violence in love. Simply don't do it—even if your partner seems to want you to hit them or openly asks you to.

Inflicting physical pain on another may seem to provide a degree of control or a measure of relief from uncomfortable feelings for one or both of you, but it does not solve the problem; instead, it complicates the problem by adding physical pain to the emotional pain that already exists.

Verbally describing the impulse to strike your partner ("I was so angry I felt like hitting you") may accurately convey the depth of your upset feelings, but if you find yourself saying it a lot, you need to examine your beliefs about hitting as a solution to frustrating feelings.

There's no such thing as an uncontrollable temper, although there are people who haven't learned to control their tempers or to express anger constructively. But you don't usually find them in lasting love relationships.

Never express angry feelings in a physical way.

HURT

When you do hurt your partner unintentionally, it may help to say, "I'm sorry," but you should not be lulled into thinking that this completely repairs the damage. Each incident gets added to the effects of the previous ones. A pattern of hurt can lead to a significant loss of love.

The most effective way to repair inadvertent hurts is to say you're sorry, state your intention not to do it again, and follow through.

> *Never aim to hurt; you'll hurt each*
> *other enough unintentionally.*

HURT

As a child, you may have tried to hurt a person you blamed for hurting you. And if you were successful, you may have felt some momentary relief and satisfaction that the score had been evened. Unfortunately, if you carry this way of dealing with hurt into your adult relationships, whatever momentary satisfaction it may bring is not worth the long-term deterioration it causes in the relationship.

*Avoid the temptation to ease your hurt
feelings by getting even with your partner.*

RESENTMENT

Resentment is one of the most common problems in a long-term relationship, usually resulting from one of you feeling that you always get the short end of the deal. If you don't deal with your resentments in a direct way, they are likely to affect your overall attitude toward your partner and keep any positive feelings from being felt or expressed. So while on the surface this may not seem as serious as some of the more obvious emotions, it can work like a cancer in killing your relationship over time.

The reason your feelings of resentment can be so powerful is that they usually reflect your feelings about other issues in your relationship, such as fairness and equality or power and control. It won't do any good to focus only on whatever specific areas of your relationship reflect the unfairness. While the specific areas can serve as illustrations of the problem, you must also deal with the general issue of fairness between the two of you.

> *Don't underestimate the power of resentment to affect your relationship*

RESENTMENT

If you feel that your partner has things better than you, you need to question whether this is because of your partner's actions or your own. In most cases, it's both; you collude and cooperate (perhaps unconsciously) in creating a situation where one of you gives up too much for the other—and then resents it.

Thoughtfulness and sensitivity can backfire if you judge your partner as bad for enjoying the benefits of your generosity. You might question if you acted out of love or out of an effort to control or manipulate your partner. If you acted only to get a certain response and then failed to get that response, you may feel resentful. But you can more effectively deal with these feelings if you take responsibility for your part in creating them instead of placing all the blame on your partner.

Be sure you don't set yourself up to feel
resentful by failing to take care of yourself.

CRITICISM

In general, criticism does more harm than good, because criticism is usually based on a fantasy image of the perfect person. You may kid yourself that constructive criticism is a good thing, but criticism is almost never seen as constructive by the person to whom it's directed. Few people make any significant changes in response to criticism. They need encouragement and support, not criticism, if they are to be all they can be—which never means being perfect.

Criticizing your partner is usually a sign of your desire to control your partner, and most people will resist what they perceive as a power play. Your partner is likely to react to these efforts with resistance and defensiveness, not by making whatever change you are suggesting.

> *Never measure your partner by*
> *some ideal, unrealistic standard*

CRITICISM

There's probably nothing that will dampen your partner's sexual ardor more quickly than judging their appearance or their sexual performance. Don't do it. Remind yourself that judging has a very low likelihood of improving things.

Showing appreciation for your partner's body will do more to motivate them to care for their body than any criticism can ever do.

Never judge your partner sexually

JEALOUSY

One of the first things that happens when a relationship gets serious is that one or both people start to feel jealous or possessive. The time to deal with these feelings is immediately.

At first, you may be flattered by your partner's jealousy—or your partner may love the idea that you want to be a part of everything they do. But these feelings quickly turn to irritation and can cause a great deal of friction between you.

Avoid the temptation to make your partner jealous as a way of extracting something from them or, worse still, punishing them. It may seem harmless enough, but it is not an effective way to get your partner to say "I love you."

Be alert to feelings of possessiveness or control.

JEALOUSY

No one can satisfy all the emotional needs of another. It's perfectly OK and even desirable for both you and your partner to have other close friends. You need them to discover more fully who you are and to realize more of your potential. Avoiding close relationships with anyone except your partner not only shuts off important avenues of personal growth, but also greatly increases the possibility that your primary relationship will eventually become boring.

Far from being harmful to your primary relationship, close friends can enrich it and take some of the pressure off you and your partner to meet all of each other's relationship needs.

To avoid arousing feelings of jealousy and animosity,

- ❧ keep your partner well informed about your other relationships,
- ❧ never make unfavorable comparisons between the relationships, and
- ❧ include your partner on occasions when it's appropriate.

> *Develop other close relationships with both men and women, and encourage your partner to do the same.*

JEALOUSY

Jealousy is closely related to fear, primarily the fear of losing your partner. As with any kind of fear, it grows stronger when you try to hide it from others.

So it's important to get your feelings out in the open. That does not mean you should emotionally express the way you feel; it means you need to describe your feelings to your partner.

Bringing these dark feelings out into the light of day is the first step in loosening their power over you and allowing you to get them under control.

Reduce your feelings of jealousy by talking about your concerns rather than hiding them or acting them out emotionally.

JEALOUSY

Check your feelings on an ongoing basis to see that you don't let jealousy or resentments interfere with your desire for your partner's happiness. If you're not working for your partner's happiness, you're probably working against it. It's important that you genuinely *want* your partner to be happy before you can support their happiness.

If you don't want good things for your partner, you need to identify the reasons you feel this way and work to change your attitude.

> *Consciously avoid letting jealousy dictate your overall feelings toward your partner.*

JEALOUSY

Most people enter new relationships with a past. You can let that past intrude on your present situation, or you can consciously and deliberately keep it in perspective. You need not ignore the past (which you couldn't successfully do anyway), but you also need not dwell on it. Try to avoid constant comparisons or competition with people from your partner's past.

People vary in their desire to know about their partner's past. While a preoccupation with the past is not healthy, a curiosity about what went into making your partner the person they are today is reasonable and can also be helpful in charting a new course together.

Deal constructively with jealousy or other complications from former relationships.

STRESS

No matter how carefully and persistently you pursue your goals and no matter how successful you are, you will experience stress. Anything that places a demand on your body or your mind is stressful. Falling in love is stressful. Having sexual intercourse is stressful. Arguing with your partner is stressful. Interviewing for a job is stressful. Being late for an appointment is stressful. The amount of stress you experience in any of these commonplace situations depends on how you view each situation, what you want from it, and the degree of loss you feel if you don't get what you want—or the amount of excitement you feel if you do.

Become aware of the stresses associated with your chosen life-style by continually identifying the things you experience as stressful. Then decide together if they are moving you in the direction you want to take or if you need to make some changes. Stress is inevitable, but it's up to you to manage the stress in your life so that it makes a positive contribution to your relationship instead of detracting from it.

Learn to manage the inevitable stress that will come your way.

STRESS

Neither you nor your partner is likely to deliberately make life stressful for the other, but you may inadvertently do so in the course of trying to take care of your own individual needs. Therefore, it's important to be able to talk about the stress each of you feels and the ways in which the stress is created.

The attitude with which you discuss this issue (whether in a problem-solving way or a judgmental way) will dictate the effectiveness of this kind of sharing.

Engage your partner in identifying
the ways you create stress for each other.

STRESS

One of the greatest advantages to a loving relationship is having someone who is there for you, someone to whom you can turn for relief from the pressures of the outside world. Stress is an unavoidable part of life, but your ability to communicate with each other about your struggles can strengthen the bond between you and increase your ability to cope.

Join with your partner to cope with the
outside stresses that you are sure to experience

6

The Secret to
Sustaining Love

No matter how much progress you make in communicating, handling issues, and dealing with differences, you will never arrive! There will never be a point at which you can assume you've got it made. Even after 37 years of marriage, we don't take our relationship for granted. Ultimately, the key to sustaining love is recognizing that it's a process that never ends. By process we mean not a series of mechanical steps but ways of thinking and relating that become a way of life.

This shouldn't be discouraging news. The need to treat love as a lifelong process is actually the basis for the potential excitement in the relationship. It implies that the relationship doesn't need to get dull or boring. Because your interests, values, and goals are likely to change throughout your life, the ability to manage these changes and coordinate them with changes in your partner is the real challenge.

We started out with certain ideas about what our relationship *should* be, as if there were some pre-determined ideal that we could follow. Each of us felt we had chosen the "right person," but neither of us is even remotely similar to the person we were when we got together. We've finally come to see that the inherent nature of relationships is not to pursue some rigid ideal, but to engage in a sort of dance together—always flexible, forever learning and changing.

So the success of your relationship depends not on shared ideas and preferences but on such qualities as caring, the ability to grow, and a willingness to compromise. You can greatly enhance the satisfaction of your lives together if you carefully nurture these qualities.

It helps to start by being clear about the precise nature of your commitment. This involves clearly stating your attitudes and intentions. The following statements, addressing ten critical areas, can help you and your partner establish a good understanding of the basis of your relationship. This list is not a substitute for actually *doing* the things it represents. It's only a reminder of what's needed.

Committments

- ❧ I love and accept you right now—as you are and as I know you.
- ❧ I know you will change in ways neither of us can imagine, because you have virtually unlimited potential, and change is the essence of life. I will strive to support your growth, even though it may include some change that I would not choose.
- ❧ I freely choose to build a life with you that is positive for both of us and for those around us. I know this means improving the relationship skills we now have and learning new ones as needed. Our relationship is not perfect now, and it doesn't have to be. It's up to us to make it the best it can be on a continuing basis.
- ❧ I will give our relationship a high place on my agenda by committing time and energy to the work of sustaining and developing our love. I will never take it for granted and assume that it can wait while we tend to the

countless other things that will constantly compete for our time and energy.

❧ I will share with you all my thoughts, feelings, and actions that affect you and our relationship. I want and need the same from you.

❧ I will keep you informed of other significant changes in the way I view and experience my life and our life together.

❧ I will do my part to build with you a life of learning. Honest, caring communication will be our primary way of sustaining our love and learning to love more effectively.

❧ I know that neither of us can meet all the needs of the other. I will work with you to find the right balance of time together and time apart so that we can each satisfy some of our important needs with others and in separate activities. I know that this balance will change over time as our life circumstances and the world around us change.

❧ In committing ourselves to the building of a life together, we are each giving up some of the freedom we had when living alone, and we are gaining the tremendous benefits of facing life's vicissitudes from the vantage point of a solid partnership. I welcome your support, and I will be there for you in difficult times.

&. I will consciously seek to add fun to our lives as long as we're together. Life is challenging enough without our taking ourselves and our circumstances too seriously.

Don't just read this list and then tuck it away. Live it on a day-to-day basis. You don't have to memorize the items and check them off as you do them, but recognize that each point is based on the theme of maintaining a positive attitude toward each other and toward your relationship. This chapter will discuss the specific ways of demonstrating this positive attitude—through caring, seeking balance, making trade-offs, learning, and growing together.

CARING

You'll be amazed at the impact of pleasing your partner in small, simple ways. Just as petty problems can add up to dissatisfaction, little touches of thoughtfulness can add up to positive feelings between the two of you.

The overall degree of closeness you feel will be greatly affected by the seemingly insignificant acts of daily life. Constant griping and pettiness will drive you apart while simple gestures of caring will draw you closer together.

> *Pay attention to little everyday gestures*
> *of kindness and consideration.*

CARING

Your partner will sense the genuineness of your caring, so be sure you're acting out of love and not out of trying to manipulate your partner into feeling more loving toward you. You may be able to fool them temporarily, but they will eventually realize that your caring comes with strings attached, which may cause them to resent the actions that they previously appreciated.

Since one of the core issues in a loving relationship is a sense of generosity and support, the degree to which you express genuine caring for the wellbeing of your partner will demonstrate the nature and the depth of your loving feelings.

Be genuine in your caring, not manipulative.

CARING

Supporting your partner's healthy growth (even when it's not in a direction you would choose for them) is the ultimate form of caring. Acknowledge their right to choose for themselves and strive for consistency in supporting all their efforts to develop themselves—not just the ones you approve of.

Help your partner realize their potential.

SEEKING BALANCE

Balance is an ongoing process—not an end state. Your sense of balance changes as you, your partner, and your life circumstances change.

How much is enough? This is the ultimate question which everyone must answer again and again. How much time should you spend with your partner at work, at play, with friends and other family, alone, maintaining physical fitness, reading?

When you're with your partner, how much time should you devote to making love, maintaining the relationship, planning for the future, preparing meals, improving your home, sharing recreation?

Answering these and related questions about how to spend your time and energy in ways that help you and your partner grow as individuals and as a couple is the ultimate balancing act.

Strive for balance in your use of time and energy.

SEEKING BALANCE

The effect on your relationship of your time together is greatly influenced by whether or not you include enjoyable activities in that time. If all your time together is spent focusing on problems and responsibilities, you may begin to see the relationship simply as a vehicle for taking care of business. This view of things can cause you to see the relationship itself as one of your problems.

There's validity to the old saying "All work and no play makes Jack/Jill a dull boy/girl." The same kind of imbalance can make a relationship dull as well. So don't think for a moment that pursuing pleasure together is frivolous; it's an essential ingredient of a healthy relationship.

Allow time for joint pleasures,
not just joint responsibilities.

SEEKING BALANCE

Fully enjoy life's daily activities. You have everything you need to enjoy every day. Use your imagination.

Linger under a warm shower. Pay attention to the way the water feels as it pounds your skin.

Take a long walk—not to go to a particular place, but just for the pure enjoyment of it. This kind of activity is good for your body as well as your spirit

Enjoy the simple pleasures

SEEKING BALANCE

If both of you are convinced of the value of time together *and* the value of time apart, the trick is to find the right balance.

In most relationships, one person wants more time together than the other one. Unfortunately, you may assume that the one who wants more time together loves more than the other. This is seldom the case. There are many reasons for wanting a lot of time together, not the least of which is our long-standing ideal of togetherness as the symbol of a good relationship. But the kind of togetherness that is stifling to the individuals is not to be desired.

Healthy relationships require enough time together for the maintenance and growth of the couple *and* enough time apart for the maintenance and growth of the individuals. Each experience contributes to the other: you will appreciate your time together much more if you have independent experiences that you can share with your partner, and you'll appreciate your time apart if you have a strong bond that allows you to venture out with confidence

> *Work toward a good balance of*
> *time together and time apart*

SEEKING BALANCE

Unless you deliberately set aside quality time to enjoy and savor your love, you may find that everything else comes first, and your love gets only whatever time (if any) is left over.

The pace of modern life doesn't automatically provide a place for love. In fact, you could probably make a good case that much of what is seen as a successful life-style today works against having an outstanding love relationship. The fast track in most organizations will absorb as much time as you are willing to commit—and often leaves little time or energy to develop a solid relationship outside the work environment. But the success that comes from devoting most of your time to work loses much of its luster if your love is the price you pay.

Children also demand a great deal of a couple's time. Before you got married you may have devoted a lot of time to simply enjoying each other's company, but the responsibilities of marriage, especially if you have children, can take up all your free time.

Sacrificing your love relationship for the sake of the kids is shortsighted. The best thing you can do for your kids is to give them parents who love each other and whose love grows stronger by devoting sufficient time to it.

Keep your priorities straight; don't
let time for love come last.

MAKING TRADE-OFFS

Don't believe those who say you can have it all. No one can have it all. You are subject to the same laws of time and energy as everyone else. When you choose one activity, you forgo another. When you choose to live in one part of the country, you rule out others.

The good news is that you are free to choose—and by setting your priorities wisely and clearly, you can probably have most of what you want. It won't necessarily be easy. If you have significant goals, you'll have to commit significant time and energy to achieving them.

> *Be realistic; realize that you can probably have anything you want—but you can't have everything you want.*

MAKING TRADE-OFFS

The trade-offs required in coordinating some activities often seem to outweigh the advantages of doing them together. Don't blame yourself or your partner for these hassles. They're a normal part of trying to build and maintain a relationship.

If you become resentful of your partner's choices or blame them for making you unhappy, you can easily develop a competitiveness and a defensiveness that make any reasonable compromise unlikely.

Acknowledge the difficulty of always finding
a good compromise when you and your
partner have different preferences.

MAKING TRADE-OFFS

When you and your partner differ, it's important to establish who feels stronger about the particular issue. A good balance in your relationship dictates that sometimes you get your way and sometimes your partner gets theirs—or that you negotiate a compromise wherein each of you makes trade-offs to achieve a mutually acceptable resolution.

While you may feel that this is a difficult process, it's actually fairly simple if both of you are dedicated to a sense of fairness. You are unlikely to successfully negotiate differences if the two of you are not committed to equality in your relationship. So addressing the underlying issues (such as fairness and equality) is essential to using the processes that will allow you to sustain your love over time.

Negotiate fairly with your partner
whenever your desires are in conflict.

LEARNING

Keep your mind alert and flexible by learning continuously from all your life experiences. You need not attend formal courses to be a lifelong learner. Simply pay attention to what's happening—including your own thoughts and the things you're observing in the larger world. Expand your understanding by listening to and learning from other points of view.

Consciously fight the tendency to become rigid in your thinking. You can only live a rich, full life by keeping your mind open to new learning and appreciating the wisdom in the saying "The more I learn, the less I know for sure."

Be a lifelong learner.

LEARNING

Your mind and your body are a package. A person with an empty mind is not very appealing. Many relationships begin with physical or sexual attraction, but for love to last, it must go far beyond this initial level of chemistry. As the excitement of falling in love wanes, your love for your partner will grow or not grow, depending on who they are as a total person—and the same is true in reverse. Love thrives on newness and is diminished by the boredom of being with someone who isn't continuing to learn.

Reading is one of the best ways to stay interested in the world—and interesting to the one you love. Treat yourself to whatever your favorite type of reading happens to be. The important thing is to exercise your mind.

Engage in conversations that do more than just pass time. Talk about things that are important to you, that you want to learn more about.

Feed your mind with good books and interesting conversations.

LEARNING

You probably were not given good books about sex and sexuality when you needed them most—as a teenager. And you may have been punished and made to feel guilty for trying to sneak a look at sexy books and magazines.

It's OK to indulge your curiosity. Go to a good bookstore or library and look at what's available. Don't underestimate the benefit you can obtain from books in the form of new information about sex and as sheer stimulation.

Learn more about improving all aspects of your life, including your sex life.

SETTING GOALS

Life is exciting when you're moving toward goals of your own choosing. Writing these goals down in a time frame with specific action plans is a good way to

- 🐾 clarify what you want,
- 🐾 increase your resolve to achieve them, and
- 🐾 track your progress.

You will increase the probability of reaching your personal goals by informing your partner of them, discussing how they fit with your goals as a couple, and enlisting their support where appropriate. Don't be dismayed if your partner doesn't share your enthusiasm for all your personal goals. It might be nice if they did, but it isn't necessary and it isn't likely.

The fact is, you may not need much active support from them, but it's still crucial that they know what you're working toward *and* that they don't feel your personal goals are a threat to your mutual goals. If they don't know your goals or if they feel threatened by them, they may inadvertently do or say things to inhibit your progress.

Be persistent in setting goals and making plans to create the life you want.

SETTING GOALS

Set joint goals with your partner and work for the best possible fit between your personal goals and your goals as a couple

Ideally, you'll have two sets of goals and plans, one for you personally and one for you and your partner as a couple. Achieving a reasonable fit between the two so that movement toward one contributes toward the other is essential to developing yourself and the relationship

> *Develop personal goals and joint*
> *goals that work for both of you*

GROWING

Change is inevitable, but growth is not. You are sure to change—and so is your partner. But growth refers only to positive change, which usually results from your deliberate efforts to change in a positive way.

You need to consciously think about the ways you want to change and how you want your relationship to change—and work toward making that happen. You can't, of course, determine how your partner should change, but you can encourage them to share their personal hopes with you so you'll know how to support their efforts.

There's risk in actively pursuing positive change. There's equal and probably greater risk in trying to hold on to the status quo. Acknowledge your fear of change and have the courage to go for the life you want.

Take responsibility for your personal growth

GROWING

The very fact that you're reading this book is clear evidence that you're already successful and that you recognize you have even more potential. No one ever realizes all their potential. This is especially true when it comes to relationships.

Few people come anywhere close to enjoying the richness that's possible in relationships. No matter what your total experience has been, it's crucial to build on your successes and know that you have the potential to build the kind of lasting, high-quality relationship you want and deserve.

Appreciate your successes and
acknowledge your potential.

GROWING

Does your partner see you as an interesting person who is exciting to be around? If not, it's time to open yourself up to being all you can be—not just for your partner's sake, but for your own. The better you feel about yourself, the more love you'll have to give. If you are to have a good balance—a good partnership—each of you needs to feel positive about who you are and where you're going in your life.

You are not likely to be satisfied (and your partner is not likely to be satisfied with you) if you deny too much of yourself for the sake of your partner or for the sake of the relationship. Remember, it's not an either-or proposition; your growth as a person increases the possibilities for growth in your relationship.

Try to see yourself through your partner's eyes.

GROWING

You may be afraid of change—either yours or that of your partner. You may think you will grow apart if you change too much. As a consequence, you may try to avoid change (which is impossible) or try to control the change so that you grow in the same direction.

Despite how much you may have heard about "growing apart" as the cause of breaking up, it's an unfounded fear. The breakup comes not because of the changes themselves, but because of the failure to communicate about the ways in which you are changing.

You and your partner don't need to avoid change or grow in the same direction in order to avoid growing apart. You simply need to stay in touch, to keep each other informed about your changes, and to support each other in the changes you choose to make.

Don't worry about growing apart; that's unlikely if you clearly communicate on an ongoing basis.

CHANGING

Don't think that after some initial period of time, you'll know all about each other. Even if you know what your partner would or wouldn't do in a given situation today, by tomorrow you might be wrong.

Each of you will continue to change throughout your life. These changes need not be seen as threatening to the relationship. In fact, you will have a more interesting, exciting relationship if you are willing to share your goals and dreams and support whatever changes they entail.

> *Accept the fact that people inevitably*
> *change throughout life.*

CHANGING

Habits are mixed blessings. They are probably essential in everyday living; good habits simplify your life by enabling you to perform routine tasks every day without really thinking about what you're doing. Habits become problems when they keep you from seeing the need to change or inhibit the process of changing.

Making love stay is not a routine task. If you depend on habit alone to sustain your relationship, it will become predictable and boring. You'll lose the excitement and stimulation that help love grow.

Anytime you say or do things in a repetitive way, you diminish their meaning and impact. Even positive actions lose their potency when you repeat them over and over in exactly the same way.

In order to sustain the level of feeling that is possible, you need to consciously change the ways you express your love to reflect the changes taking place in you and your partner. Habit can deaden your awareness and your joy. Variety and change can constantly renew your love.

> *Don't be controlled by habit; it's your*
> *worst enemy in making love stay.*

CHANGING

If you have a mental image of the ideal relationship, discuss it with your partner and work toward it, but be prepared to change course.

Love cannot be absolutely controlled, but you'll find that the love that evolves can be much better than your image of how love *ought* to be.

Don't try to force your love into a mold.

CHANGING

The essence of life is change. Nothing, not even your love, is static. Most of us have a lifelong love-hate relationship with change. We generally like it when it's of our own choosing, but we dislike it and resist it when it's imposed. But change in all aspects of life is inevitable; in fact, it's essential.

If your desire for stability and certainty are too great, you will stifle your love. But if you're open to change, you'll allow your love to thrive.

In the final analysis, lasting love is changing love.

View your love as a process—
not a thing to be possessed.

CHANGING

Since your love is always changing (with or without your conscious input), you need to stay aware of the possibilities for your relationship so you can help direct its course instead of just trying to adjust to the changes that happen.

Don't see the possibilities as limited—or they will be. Don't expect too little or settle for a narrow view of what's possible. Stay open to exploring new aspects of your love.

Take a fresh look at what's
possible for your relationship.

CHANGING

Think about how to keep your love alive and growing. Don't worry about making it last forever. Take it one day at a time.

Do something today to make it stronger.

Realize that love seldom dies suddenly;
it withers from lack of nourishment

7

Enjoying the Benefits

*T*his final chapter is devoted exclusively to the benefits of attending to all the areas of your relationship discussed earlier. It's aimed at reinforcing your excitement about investing the time and energy it takes to make your love stay. The rewards of your effort, like money wisely invested, will continue to grow and provide benefits to each of you personally and to your relationship. While you never achieve an ultimate level of these benefits, you can find incredible satisfaction as they accumulate.

So don't feel pressured to reach the next level (whatever that may be for you personally). Stop to notice the good things about your relationship today—knowing it will only get better as you continue to nourish it. You can look forward to increasing your levels of joy and satisfaction as long as you focus on making love stay and commit yourself to pursuing this path.

It's important, however, to recognize that you will not derive complete security, a risk-free relationship, total understanding, or smooth sailing. These are totally unrealistic goals based on a fearful, anxious, desperate way of viewing relationships, and now is the time to discard them. You have nothing to lose and everything to gain.

The benefits you can expect are far more rewarding: increasing levels of trust, intimacy, and loving feelings. Since these are the goals you ultimately seek, you may wonder why we waited so long to discuss them. Well, we deliberately saved these rewards till last because you really can't start with them. You don't get trust by seeking it directly. You only get it as a by-product of doing all the things described throughout the book that give rise to trust. The same is true for intimacy. Intimacy can't be forced. It emerges from the close, trusting, loving feelings that come from caring for the needs of the relationship.

And certainly lasting love doesn't come by just wanting it. It, too, comes as a by-product of the accumulation of hundreds of little thoughts and deeds throughout your lives together. This chapter connects the threads of the individual thoughts scattered throughout the book. You can't reach this point without attending to the little things that go into the whole.

Finally, this last chapter reflects on the point we made in the beginning—that the benefits of a lasting love go far beyond your relationship. A loving relationship provides a place from which to relate to the rest of the world. So we hope you appreciate and enjoy your love as you continue to find your own ways to make your love stay.

TRUST

Trust is the universal lubricant in good relationships. It produces a sense of ease, a feeling that you're accepted by the other person and therefore free to be yourself—all of yourself. A highly trusting relationship frees you to think and act with spontaneity and energy.

Conversely, in the presence of a person you don't trust, you'll tend to be guarded in what you say and do. You're unwilling to let them know you at a deep level because you're afraid of what they might do with the information. Distrust produces feelings of constraint and discomfort in its mildest forms, and anxiety and fear in its most severe forms.

It will be helpful to remember that trust is not a simple aspect of a relationship that is either present or absent. There are many degrees or levels of trust; and at any moment in time, you and your partner may hold very different views of the trust that exists between you. As your mutual trust increases, so does the potential for satisfaction for both of you.

Recognize that trust is the foundation for the things you value most in your relationship.

TRUST

Trust that's based on a deep knowing is very different from that which is typical of new relationships. Falling in love generally produces a feeling of complete trust which may or may not prove to be justified when you get to know the other person at a deeper level.

Over the life of your relationship, trust is likely to be the single most important factor in determining the amount of satisfaction you get from the relationship. Every day you're building a history of trust with your partner, and that history determines the possibilities for the future. As your trust increases, based on a deeper knowing of each other, you'll see that your initial trust was superficial in that it was based on limited information.

*Accept the level of trust that exists in
your relationship right now and know
that you can develop it further.*

TRUST

Developing high trust is a mutual endeavor with no limits. You cannot make it happen by edict and you can't control the pace at which it develops. You *can* do your part.

Don't wait for your partner to make the next move to deepen trust and don't view it as a game in which your partner must always match your actions. It won't always work that way. You may have come from a family that taught distrust, and it's not easy to overcome some of your early learnings about trust.

Be conscious and consistent in your own extensions of trust. Chances are, it will pay great dividends. If you feel your efforts are having no impact, talk about it directly, but in a constructive, nonjudgmental way.

*Show your partner how important they are
to you by constantly expanding your trust.*

TRUST

You know from your own experience that actions really do speak louder than words—especially when the two are in conflict. Be judicious in keeping your commitments to your partner.

When you break a commitment, whether consciously or unconsciously, don't offer glib excuses or try to gloss over it. Face it honestly and directly.

If it's a commitment you no longer intend to keep, own up to it and negotiate a new agreement. If it was an oversight on your part, offer a sincere apology, make amends where possible, and state your clear intention to do better next time.

> *Actively demonstrate your trustworthiness;*
> *don't just say* trust me.

TRUST

Trust is a dynamic characteristic of your relationship; it fluctuates constantly. The level of trust at any given time is a function of the attitudes, beliefs, and actions of both of you.

For your part, you sustain trust by acting with integrity—by doing what you say you're going to do and by being the person you represent yourself to be. You sustain trust by active listening—by treating your partner with dignity and respect.

But your partner has a role in this as well. Their perception of you as trustworthy is based on your actions, so your behavior must be seen as trustworthy by your partner before trust exists in the relationship. The same process, of course, works in reverse when it comes to your partner's trustworthiness.

Real intimacy and lasting love depend on each of you acting in a way that warrants the other's trust and on each of you interpreting the other's actions in a positive way.

Recognize that trust is a product
of everything you say and do.

TRUST

In the final analysis, the feelings that accompany the deepest levels of trust and intimacy are as indescribable and precious as the most powerful feelings that accompany falling in love. When you experience them, there's no doubt in your mind that this is what being fully human is all about.

Don't insist on understanding every dimension of trust.

INTIMACY

Intimacy is one of the most paradoxical of all of life's experiences. It's appealing, intoxicating, and frightening. It's both a highly charged and a deeply peaceful experience. In moments of true intimacy, you drop the normal boundaries and allow yourself to be known more completely than in any other circumstance. Deep trust is an absolute requirement for this kind of risk-taking.

Trust, intimacy, and love are inextricably intertwined. Generally speaking, as one increases, so do the other two, and when one is strong, so are the other two. Unfortunately, this is not always the case. It's possible to love someone a great deal, but not trust them and therefore refuse to be intimate with them. This most often occurs when trust is broken.

Broken trust can be repaired, but it can't be done quickly. Rebuilding trust calls for gradually establishing a pattern of trustworthy actions.

> *Take the risks that are inevitable in deep trust; it's the key to real intimacy.*

INTIMACY

It's not possible to schedule intimacy like you would a meeting, but you can create the conditions for intimacy by making yourself available to your partner in a timely way. You enhance the prospects for intimacy when you set aside the time and initiate the kind of sharing that invites your partner to reciprocate. The benefits of intimacy for your relationship as well as for your life as a whole are enormous.

The degree of intimacy you enjoy will vary, and there are easily identifiable reasons for these fluctuations. Problems in your relationship may cause you or your partner to feel too distant or distrustful to engage in intimacy. You or your partner will have periods when you are distracted by work, family matters, or other problems and simply not available to each other. It's in your mutual best interest not to pursue such distractions to the point where you ignore their impact on your time and availability for each other.

Consciously make yourself
available for intimate contact.

INTIMACY

From time to time, you are likely to be aggravated by differences of opinion or ways of doing things; that's inevitable in dealing with the many details of daily living. Naturally, you won't feel as close to your partner in the midst of a disagreement, but you can minimize its impact on your trust and intimacy in two ways:

- 🐾 First, you need to keep the perspective of what's really important in your relationship and not let any single issue take on more meaning than it deserves. The benefits of intimacy are too valuable to let them be affected by every changing mood.

- 🐾 Second, you need to express your feelings and perceptions in a constructive, timely way so that you don't accumulate them until they add up to a big load of resentment. The advice to "never go to bed angry" is far too simplistic in its scope, but its intent (to recognize the importance of protecting your intimacy) provides a valuable perspective.

Don't allow the daily trivia to erode
your trust and block intimacy.

INTIMACY

Give sex its rightful place in your life as a loving couple. Sex is more than just a physical act or a symbol of an emotional commitment. At its best it's part of the spiritual bond between you that provides a solid place to stand in the world.

If you see sex only as a diversion from the normal business of living, you'll lose much of the potential benefit.

Make sex an integral part of
your life, not an isolated activity

INTIMACY

Outstanding sex requires that both you and your partner expose your feelings and emotions in great depth to each other. Allowing another to see and know you that intimately may feel threatening, but it's the only way to reach the potential that exists in the sex act.

Take the risk. Extend the trust to your partner, and in turn, treat their personal disclosures with tenderness and respect. And you need to listen carefully for whatever concerns your partner may have about being vulnerable with you.

Good sex thrives when you feel safe enough to be completely open about your thoughts and feelings.

Be willing to be vulnerable.

INTIMACY

The payoff for the time you devote to enriching your love goes far beyond the satisfaction that comes from having a great relationship. It can provide moments of peace when all the normal problems of the world disappear from your awareness.

The experience of oneness and peace that comes at the climax of a good lovemaking session is one of the finest parts of a loving relationship. Those moments are precious, and it's clear the feelings that follow loving sex are far deeper and more significant than the feelings produced by the sexual act per se. When you're basking in those feelings, time stands still.

Make time stand still.

LASTING LOVE

Learn to love your partner—regardless of their behavior. This doesn't mean you have to love every part of your partner's behavior. It does mean you continually acknowledge them and affirm your love, despite their behavior at the moment.

When your partner experiences this kind of love, they may react with surprise, since most people are accustomed to love with strings attached. Keep up your unconditional love and watch your partner grow from it.

Love unconditionally.

LASTING LOVE

Care for your love like the living thing that it is. Attend to its needs. Give it room to grow. Feed it nourishing things. Protect it from harm. Surround it with a supportive environment.

Take time to enjoy your love. Handle it like a butterfly; welcome it, but don't frantically pursue it, and don't grasp it. Hold your love lightly. Don't let it slip away unnoticed.

> *Give your love lots of time and*
> *attention; never take it for granted.*

LASTING LOVE

Every love relationship is special in that it's the result of the combined feelings of love of two unique individuals.

You don't need to question how your love measures up against anyone else's. You can't know what some other love feels like to the people involved, and they can't know how yours feels to you.

So focus only on your own relationship and appreciate the wonderful feelings that are possible for you!

*Savor the specialness of your love
relationship; it's like no other.*

LASTING LOVE

Your love doesn't exist in isolation; it's part of your total world. You need to stay in touch with all the wonderful things in the world that give meaning to your life.

By integrating your love for other special things in life with the love you feel for your partner, you can develop a loving way of being in the world. Your love is likely to stay when it becomes a way of life.

Be open to the wonders of the world around you.

About the Authors

Authors of three other books, including the best-selling *The Monogamy Myth*, Peggy Vaughan and James Vaughan, Ph.D., are a husband and wife consulting team specializing in relationships between women and men. As frequent guests on national television and radio programs, they back up their professional expertise with a willingness to speak about their personal experiences as a couple. Currently living and working in La Jolla, California, the Vaughans have been married for 37 years. For the last 20 of those they have worked with couples to help their love last.